Introduction.

Within the pages of this poster book you will find over 50 high quality vintage images of Angels, Fairies, and Cherubs from the Victorian era.

These beautiful illustrations would look great either cut out and framed or, just enjoyed as they are presented here in this publication.

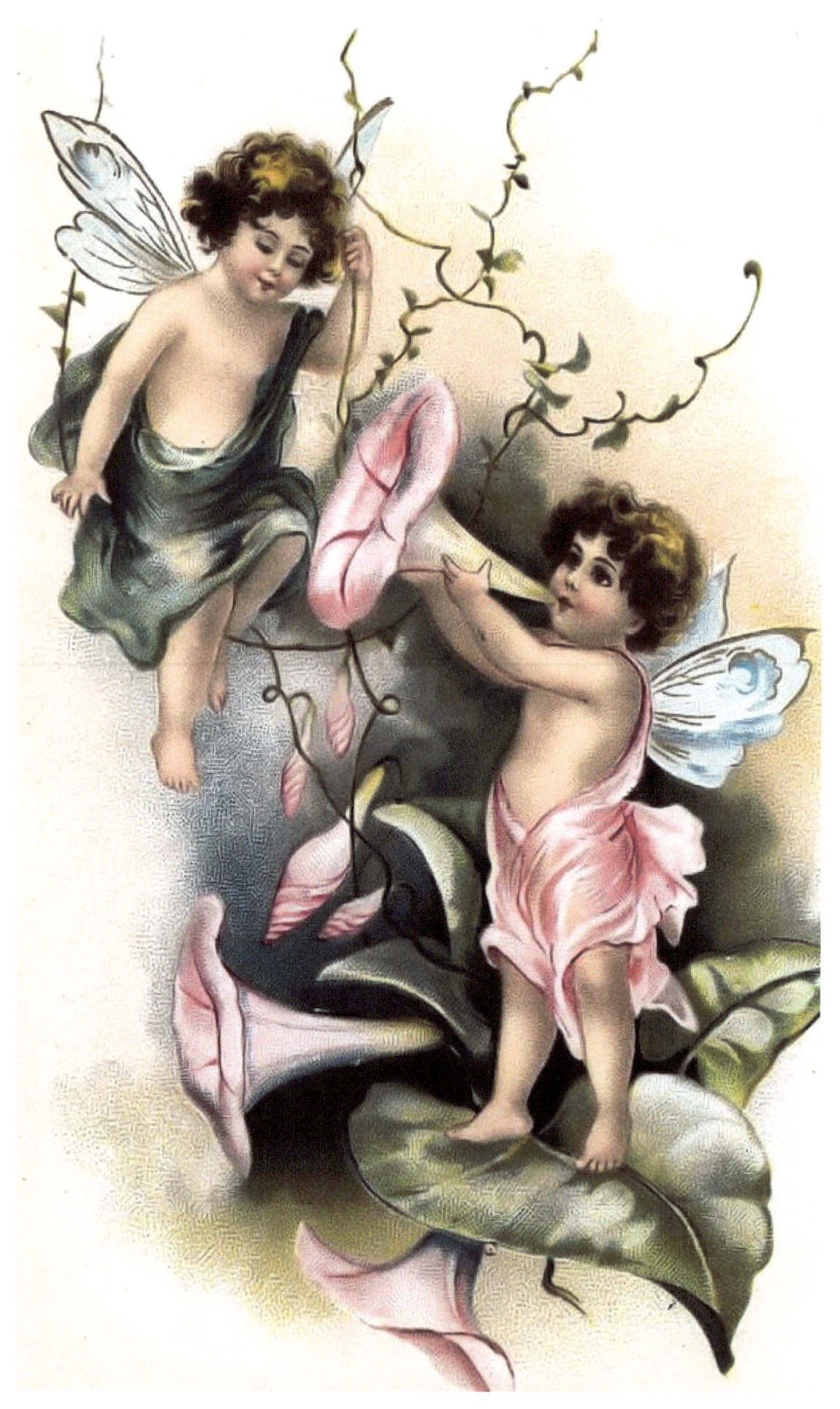

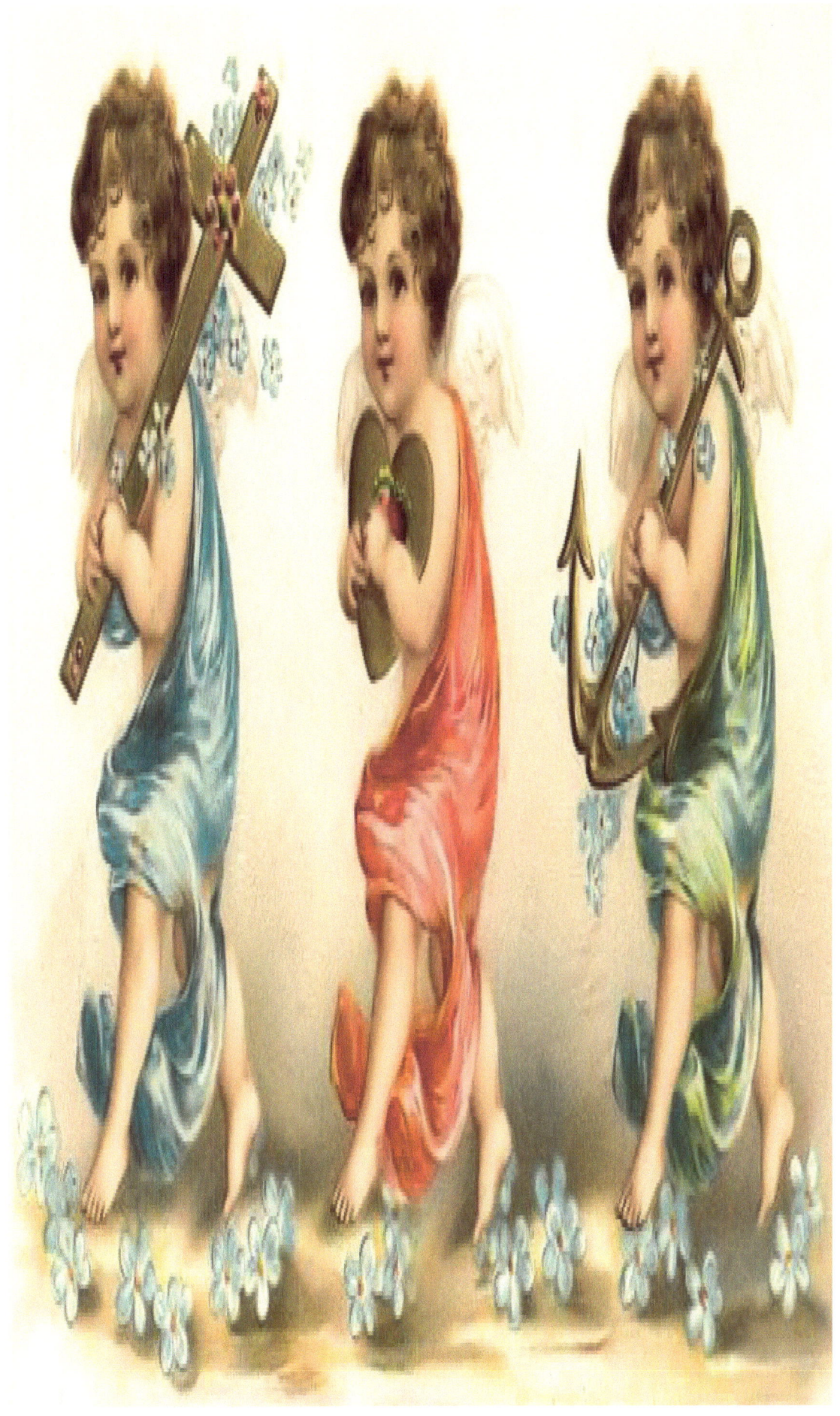

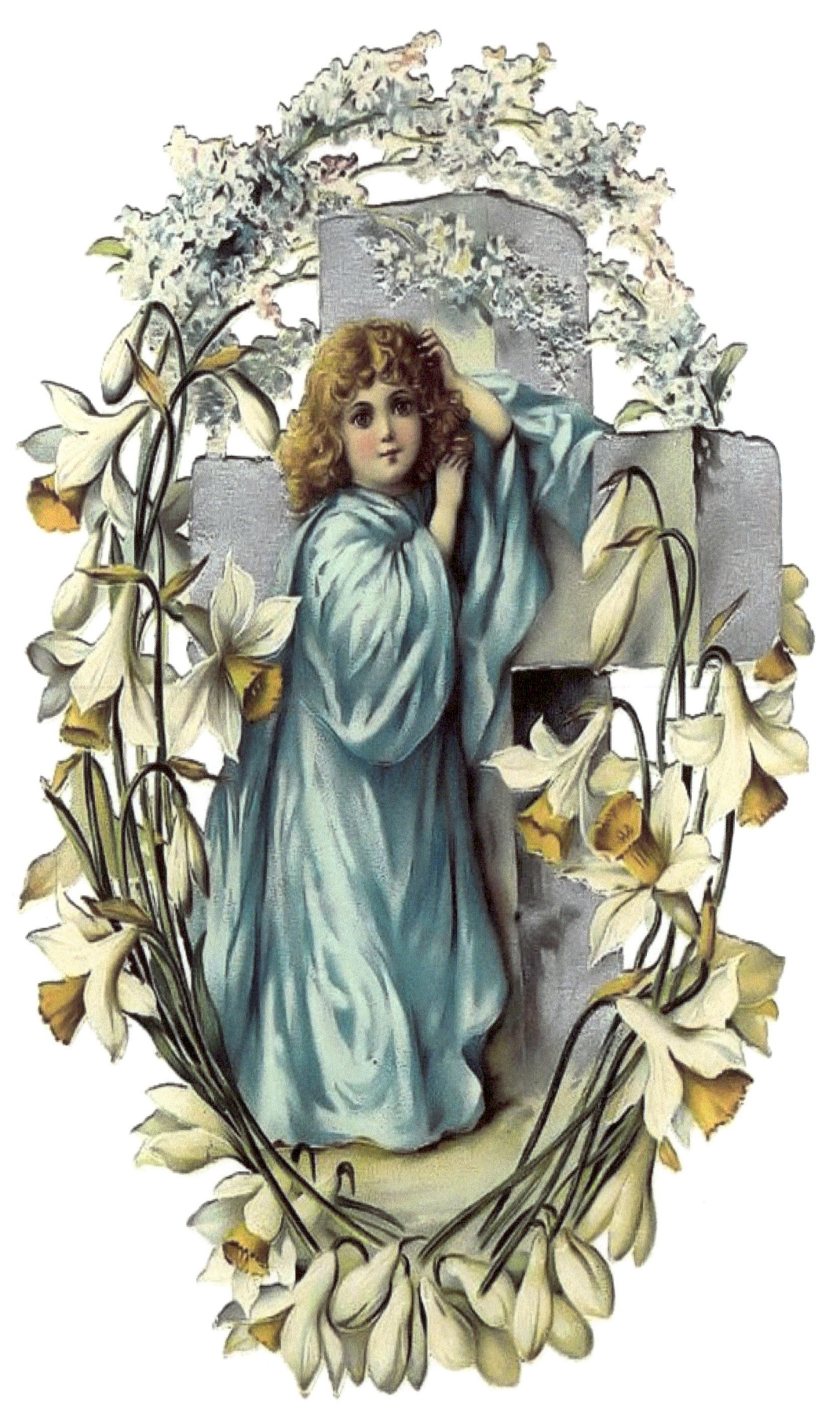

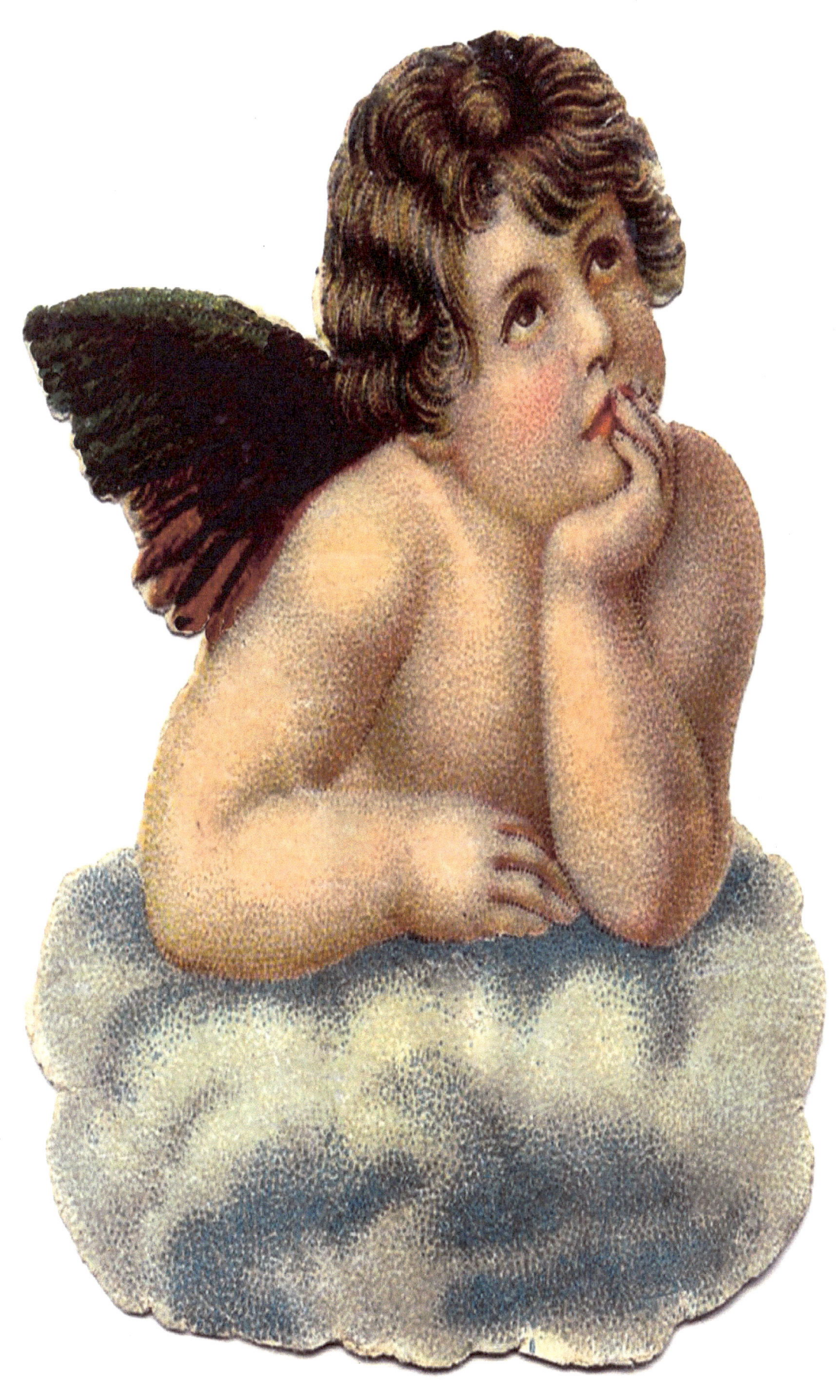

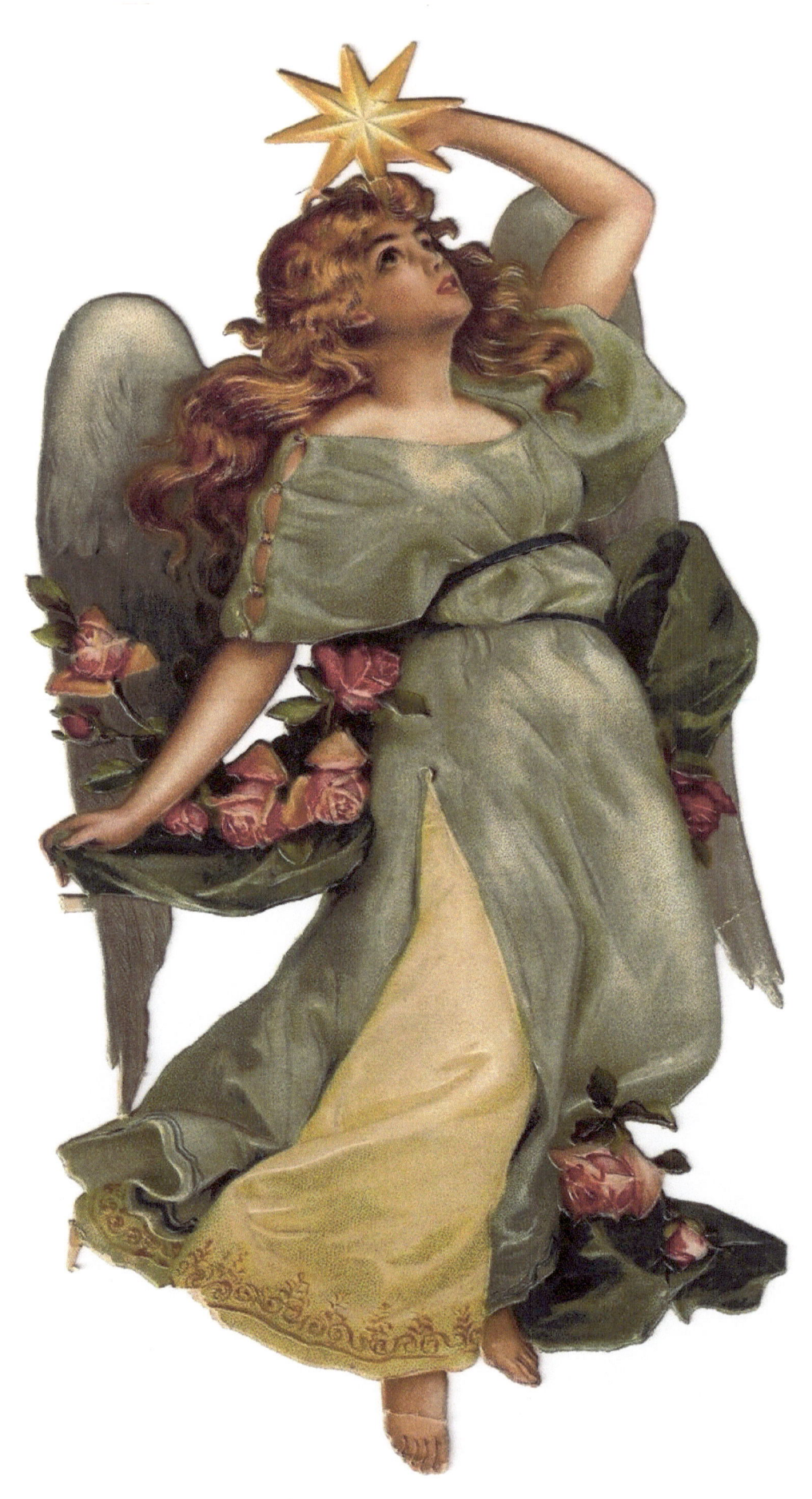

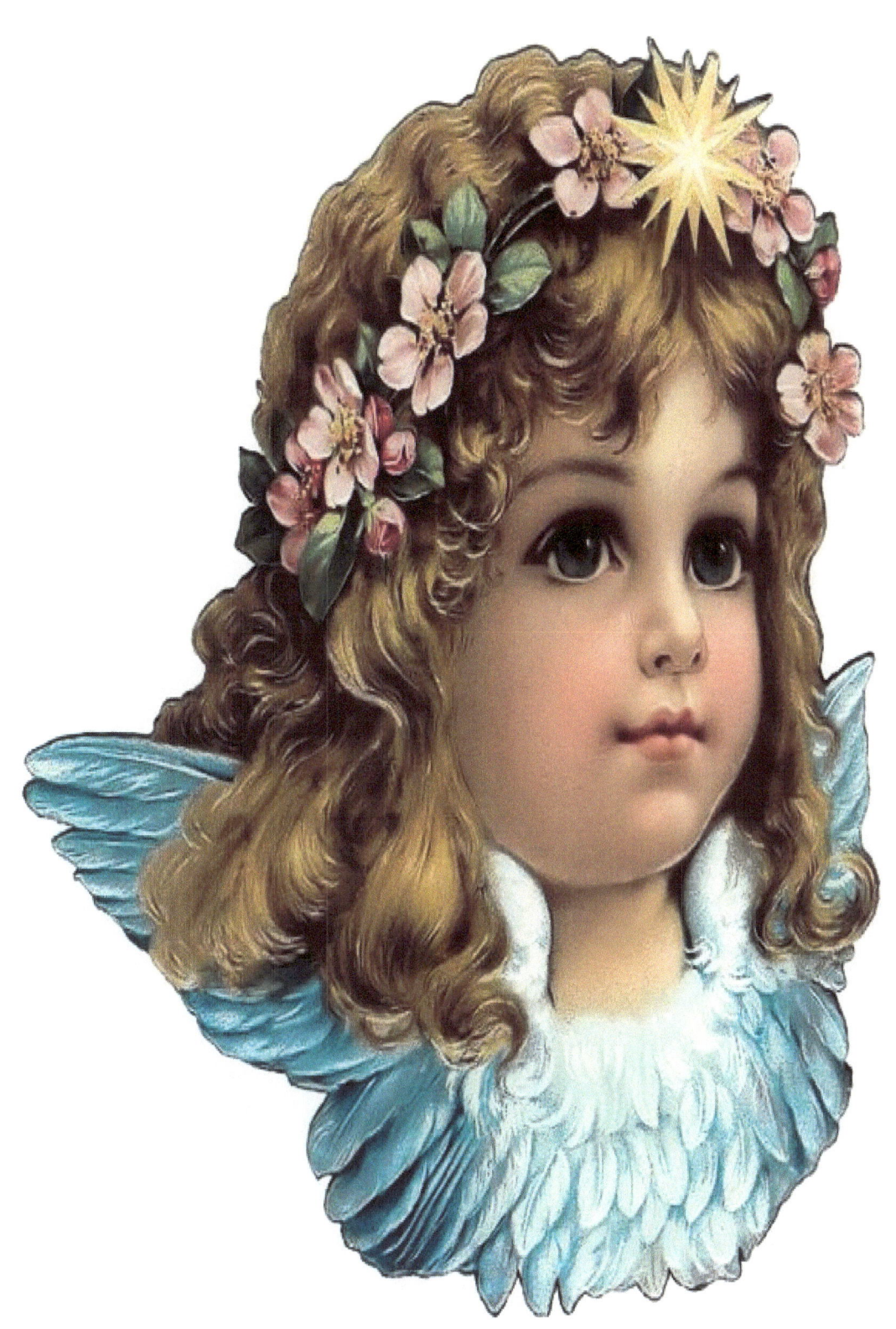

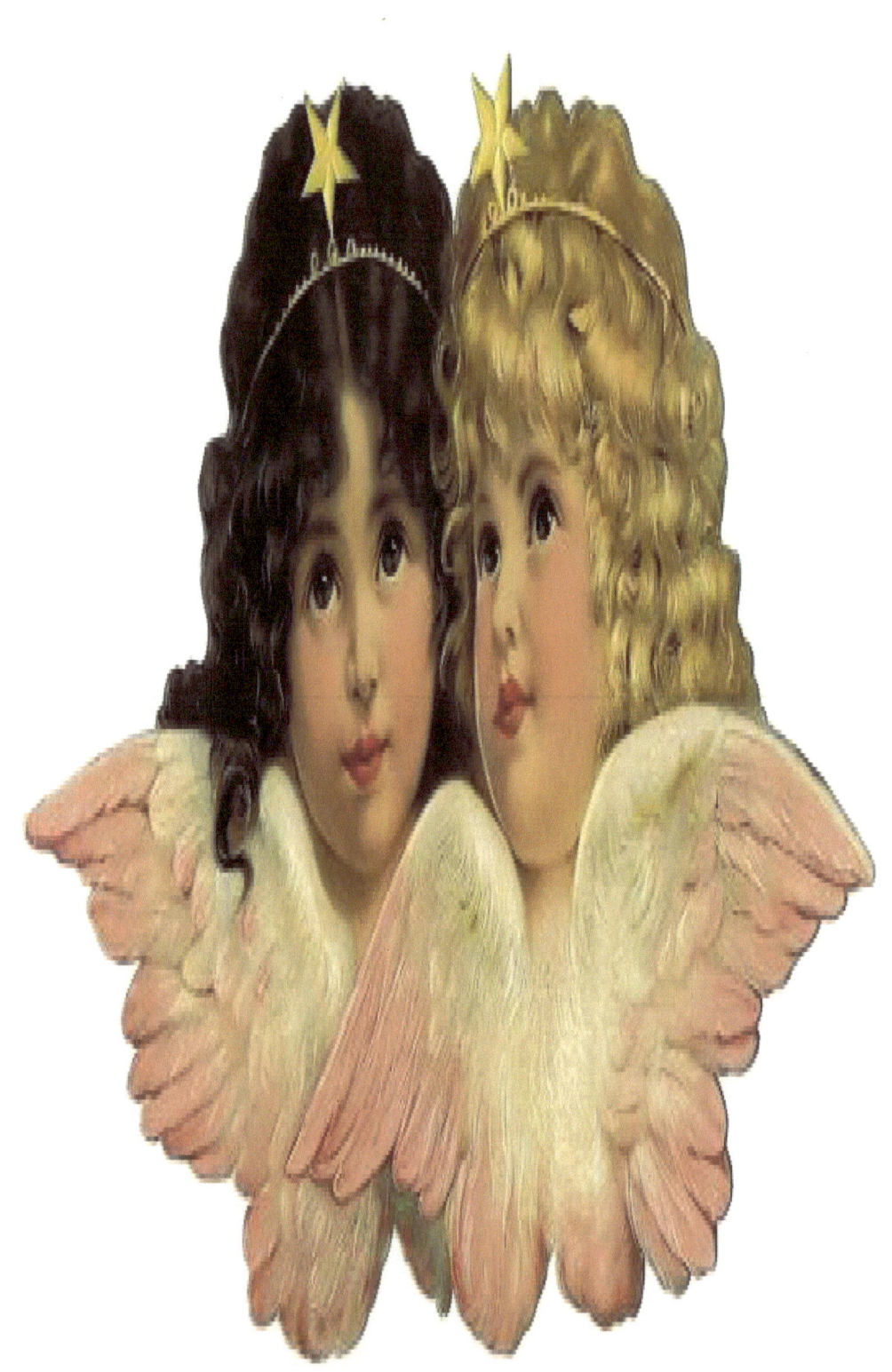

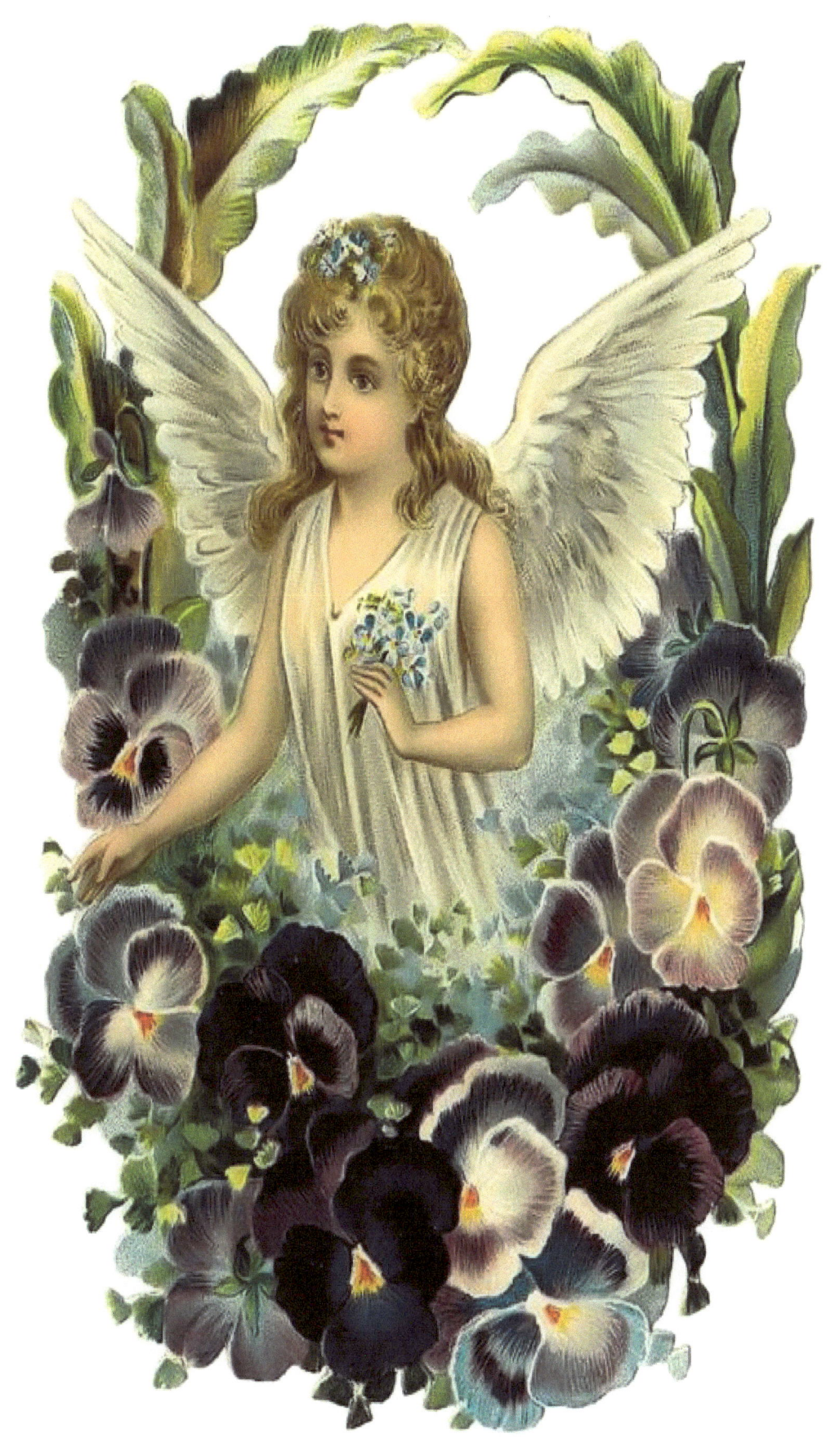

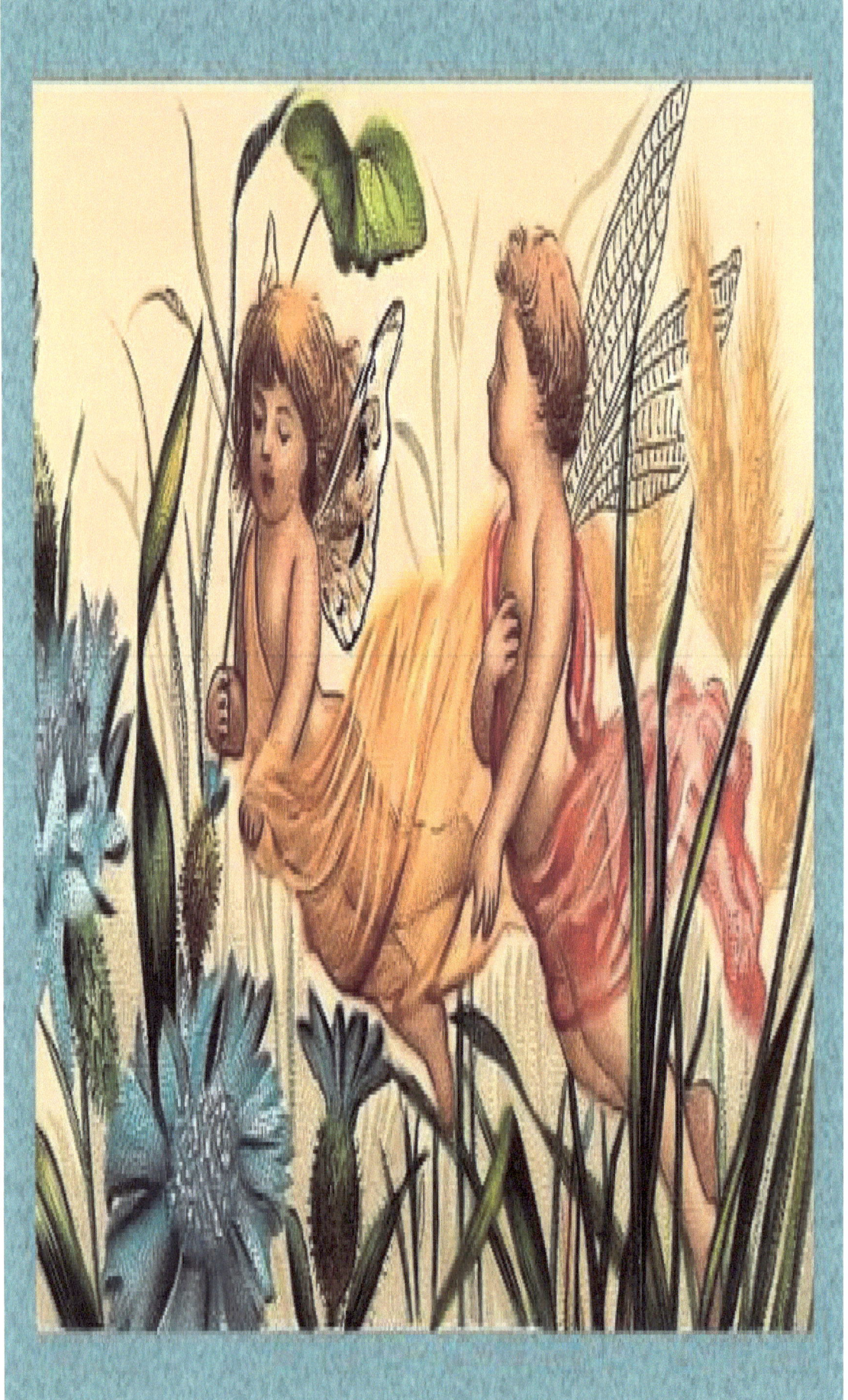

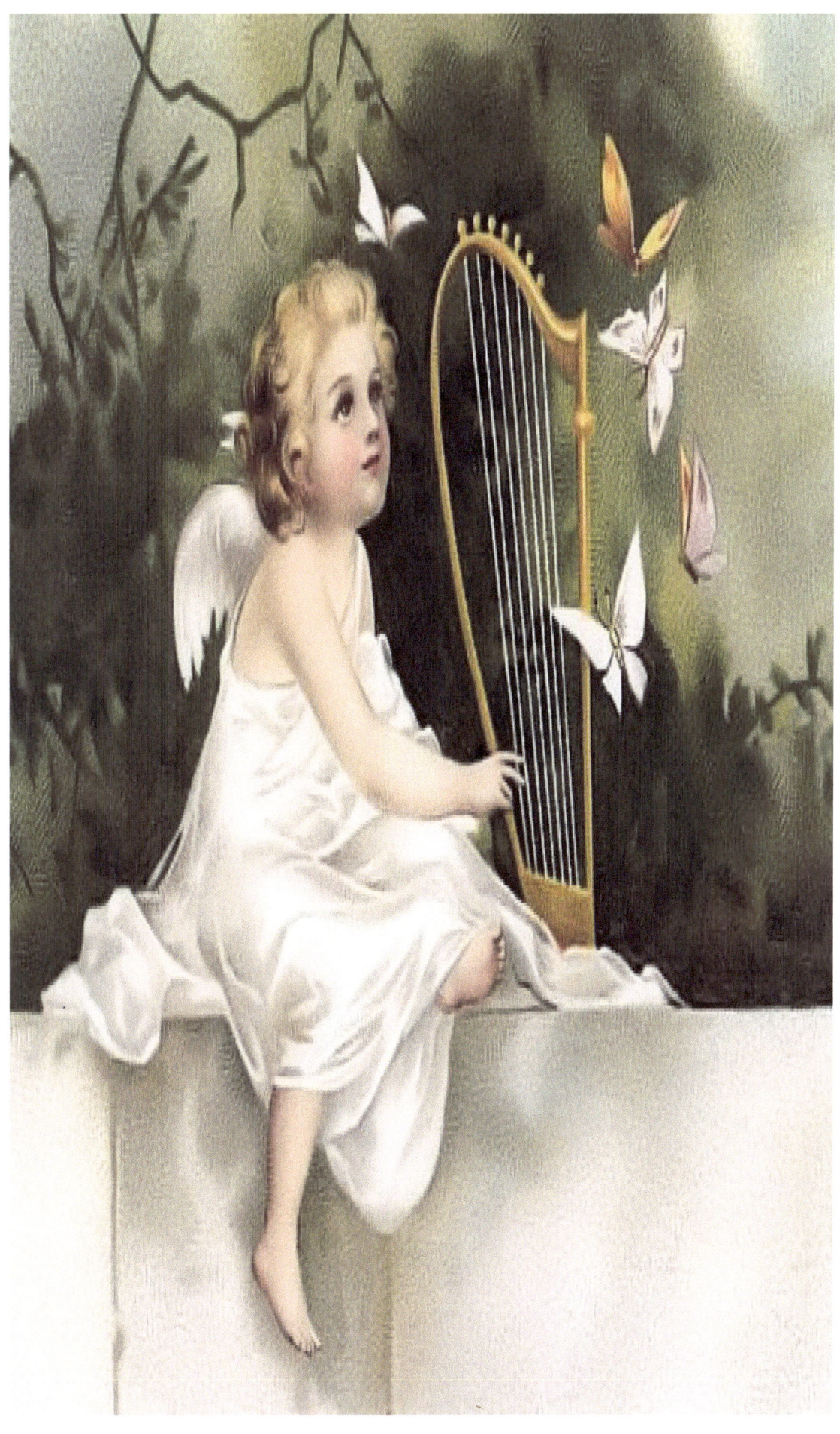

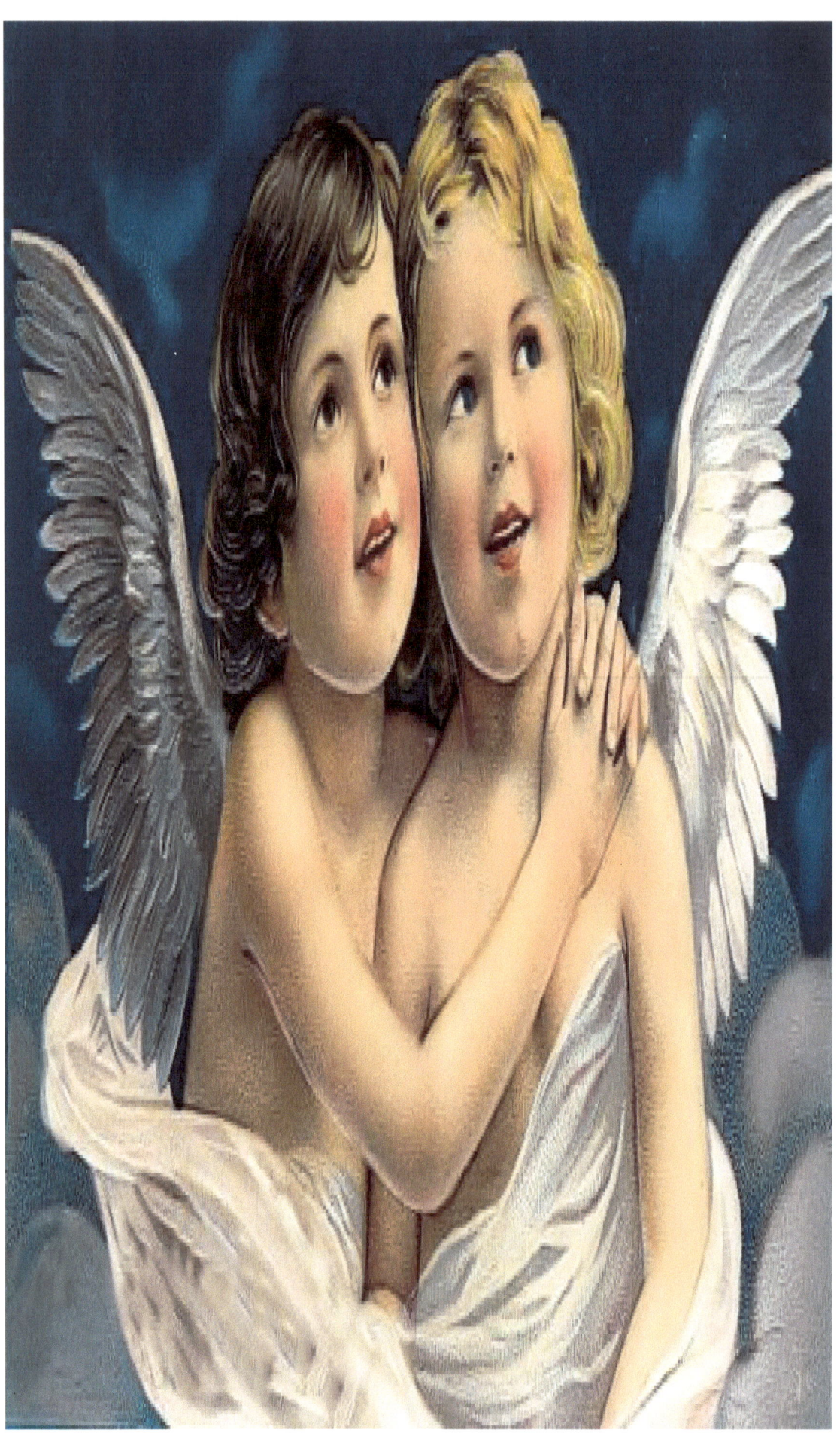

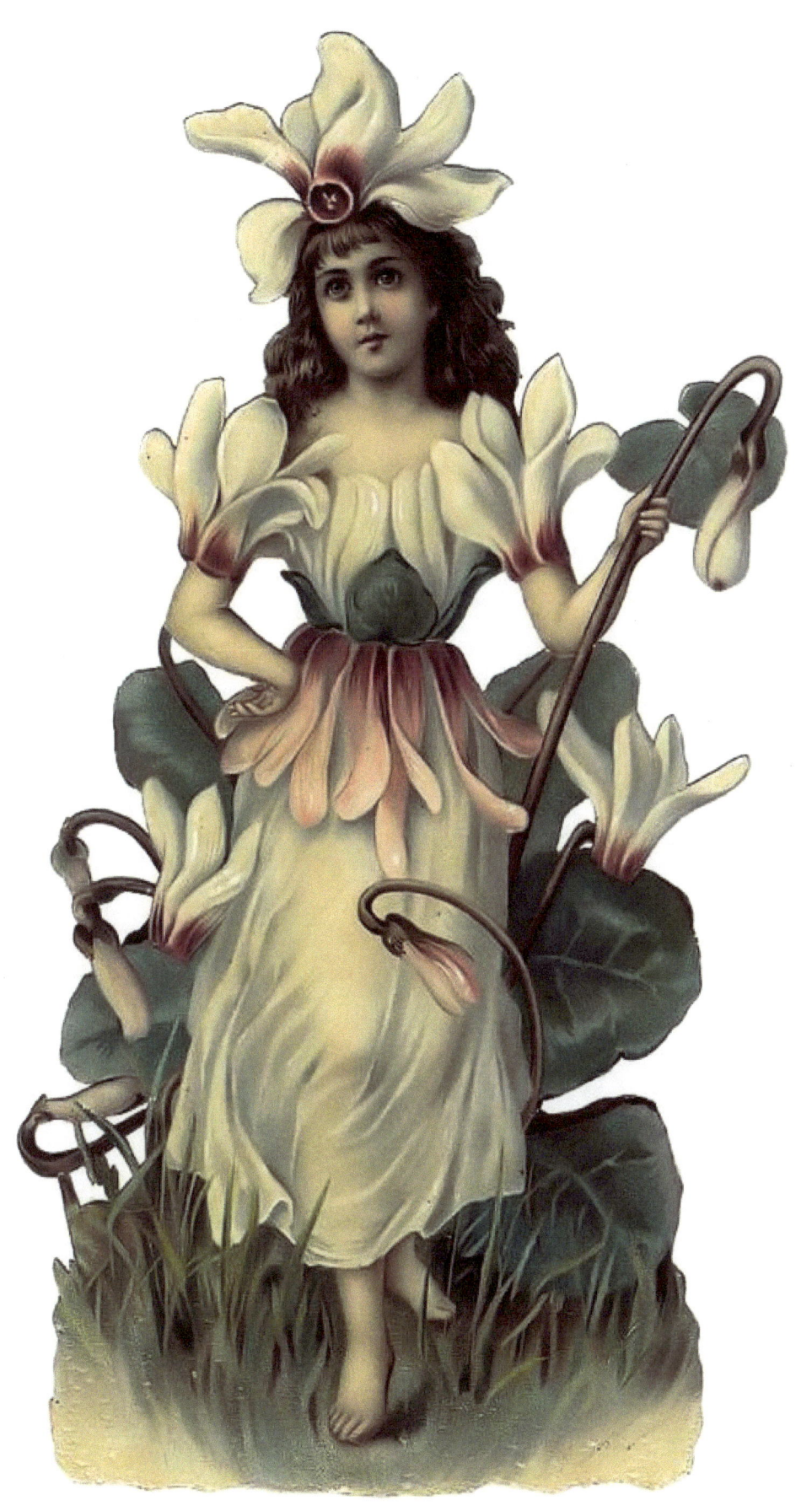

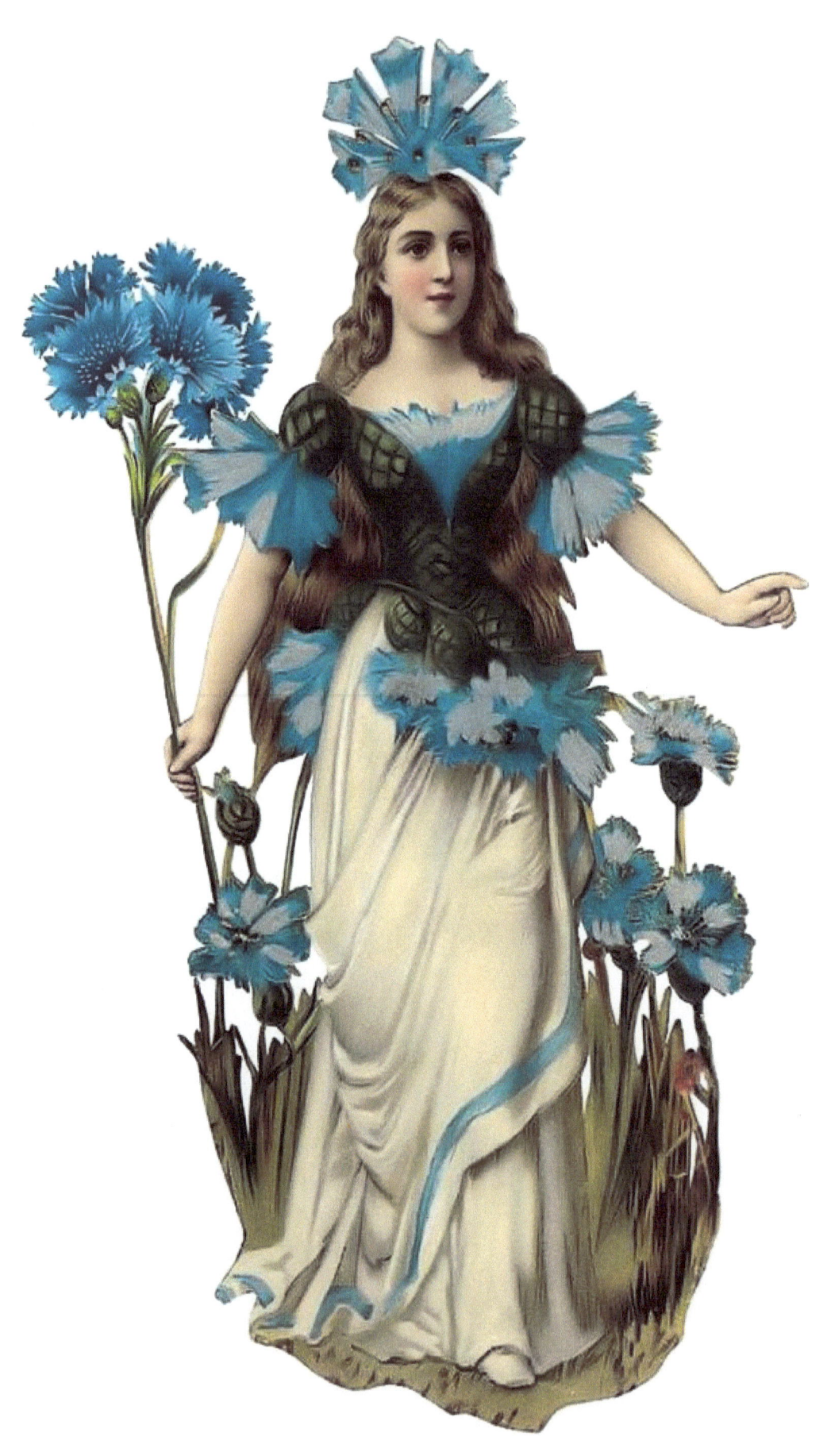

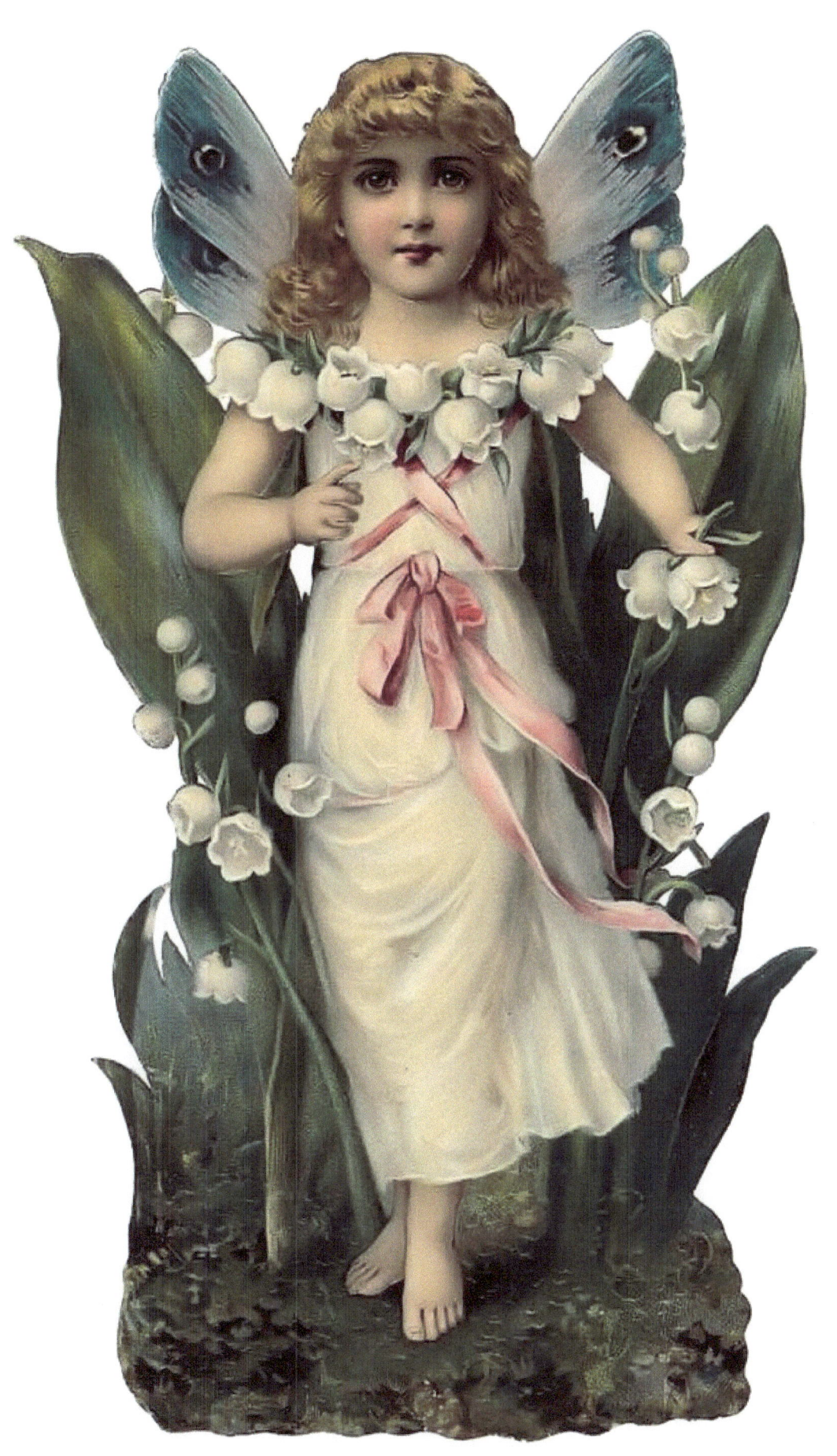

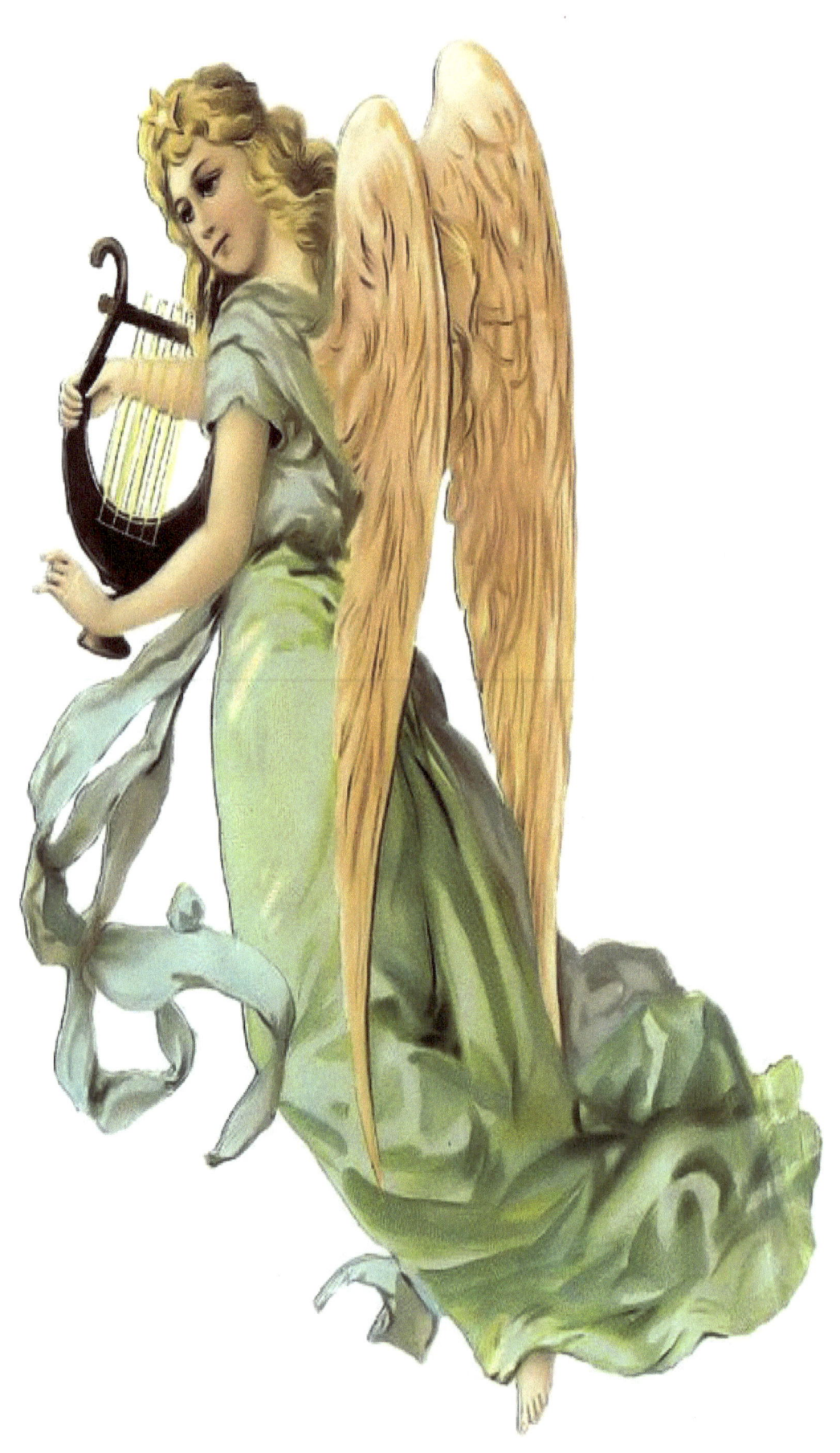

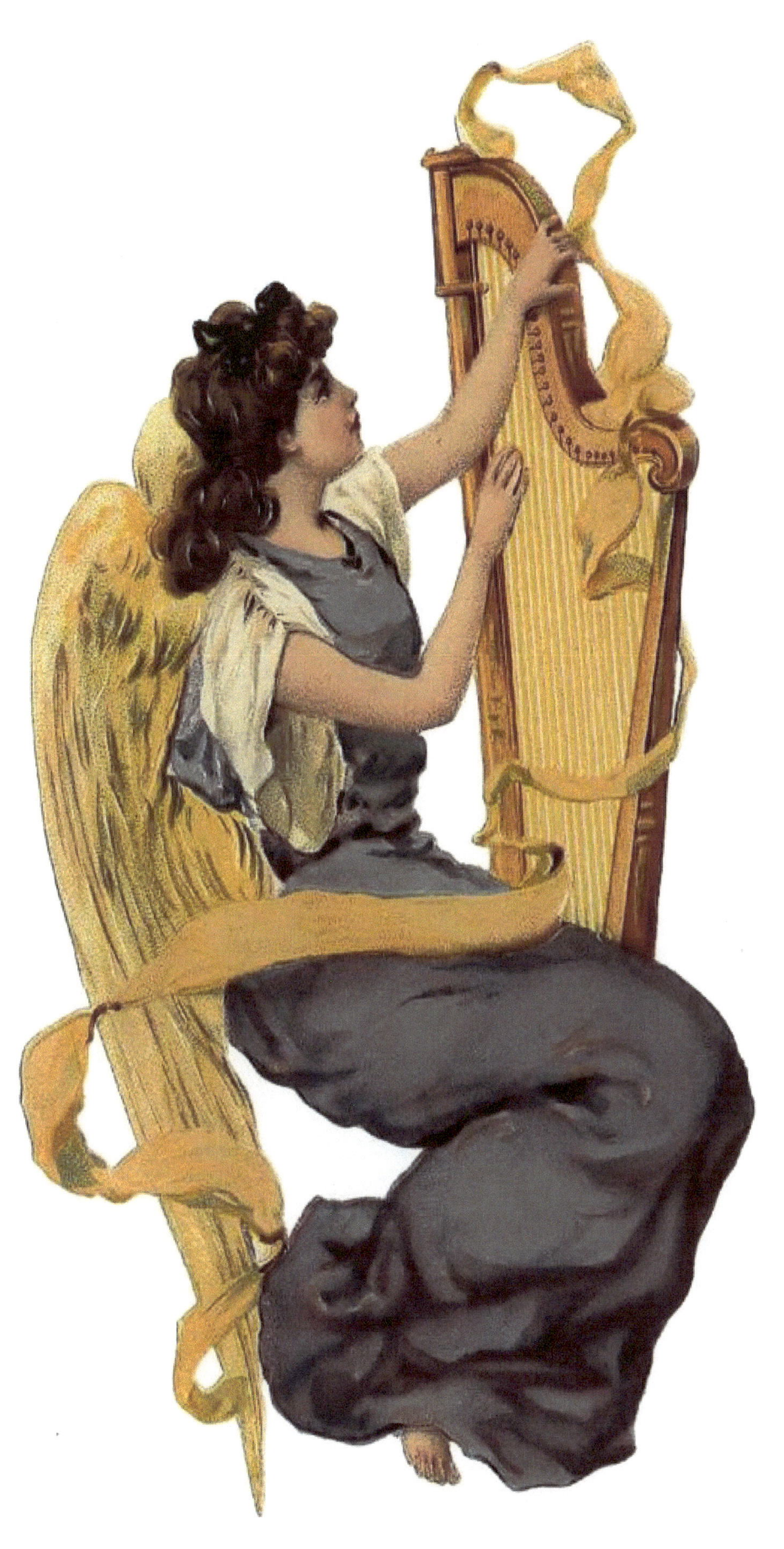

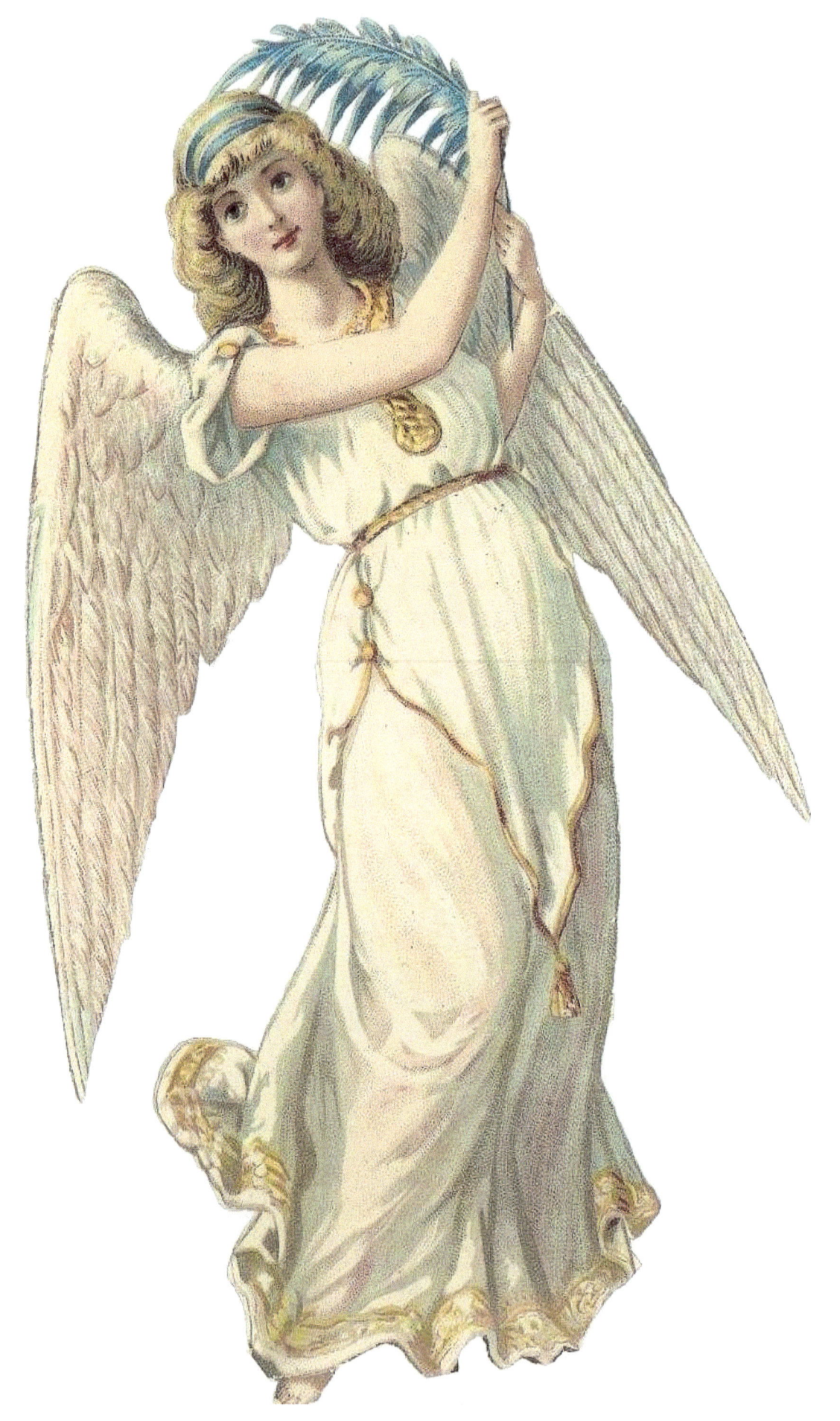

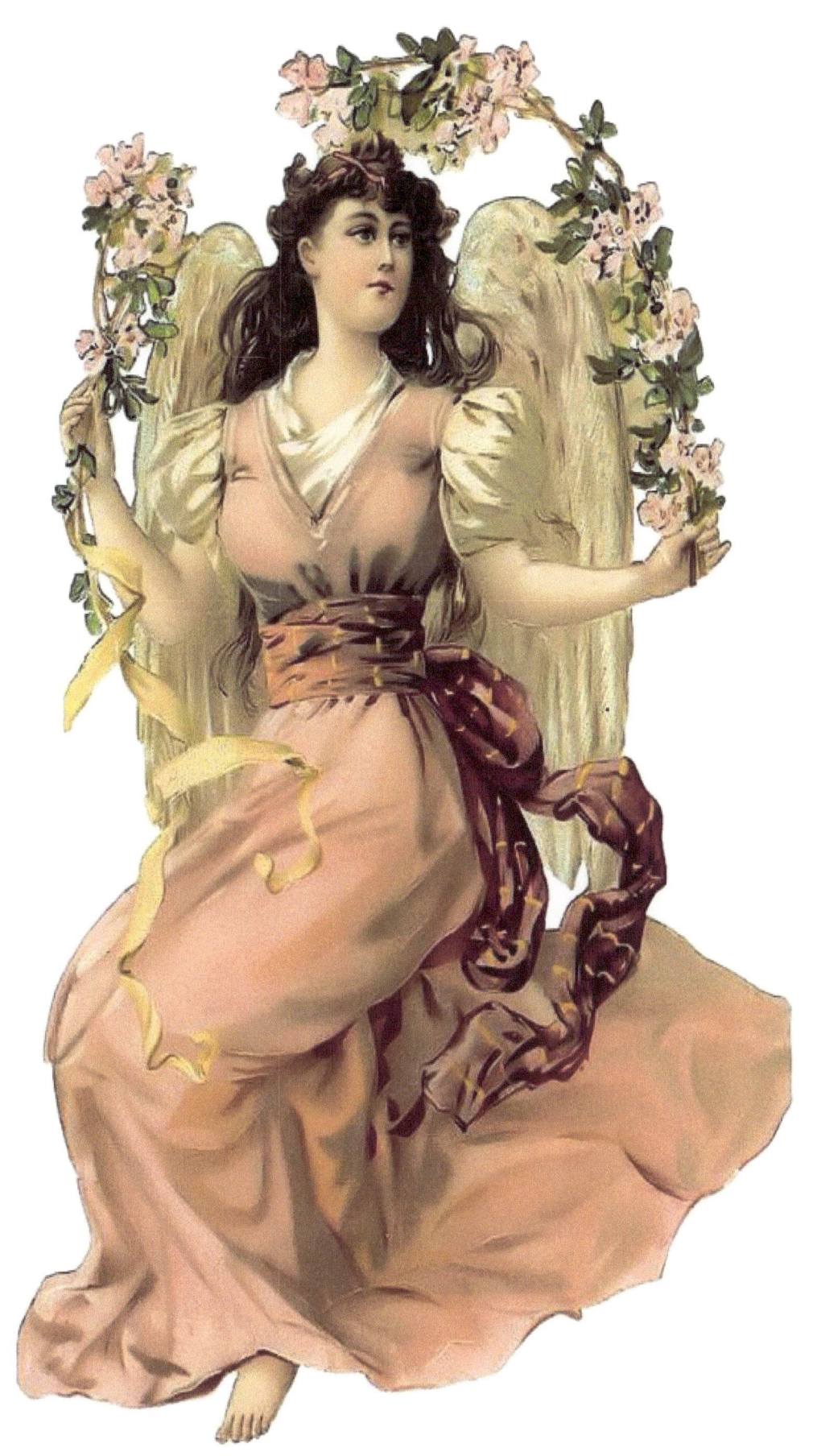

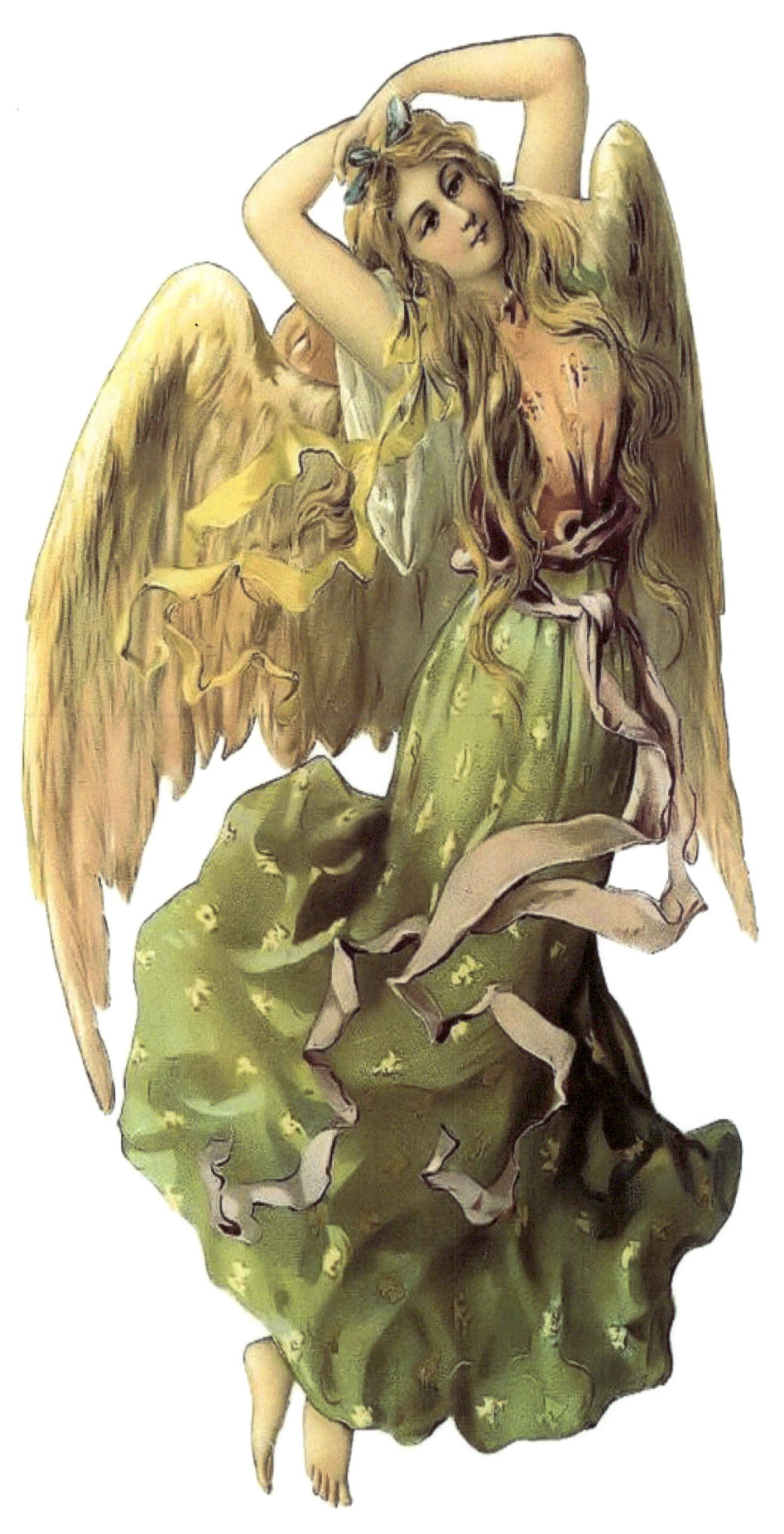

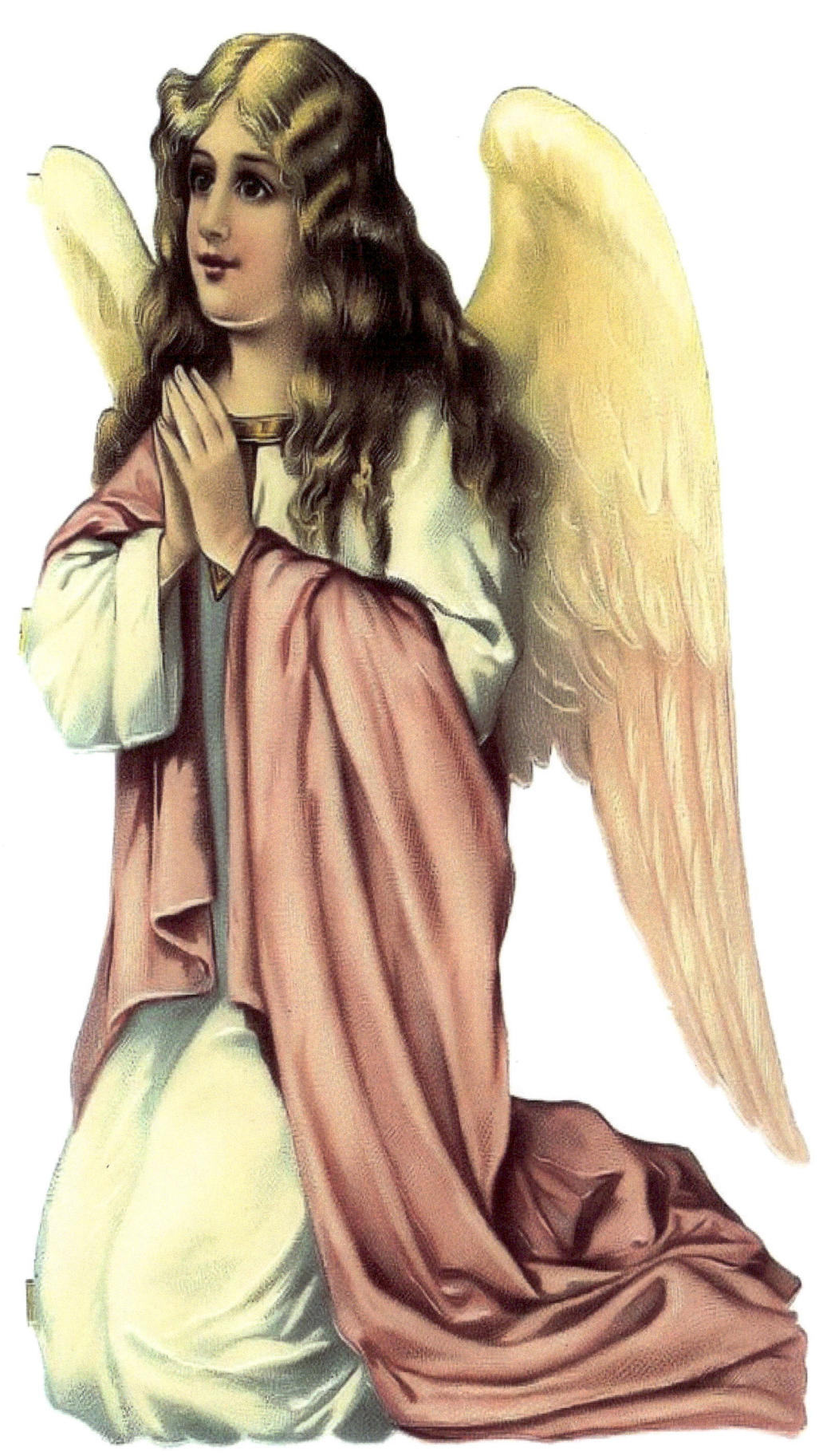

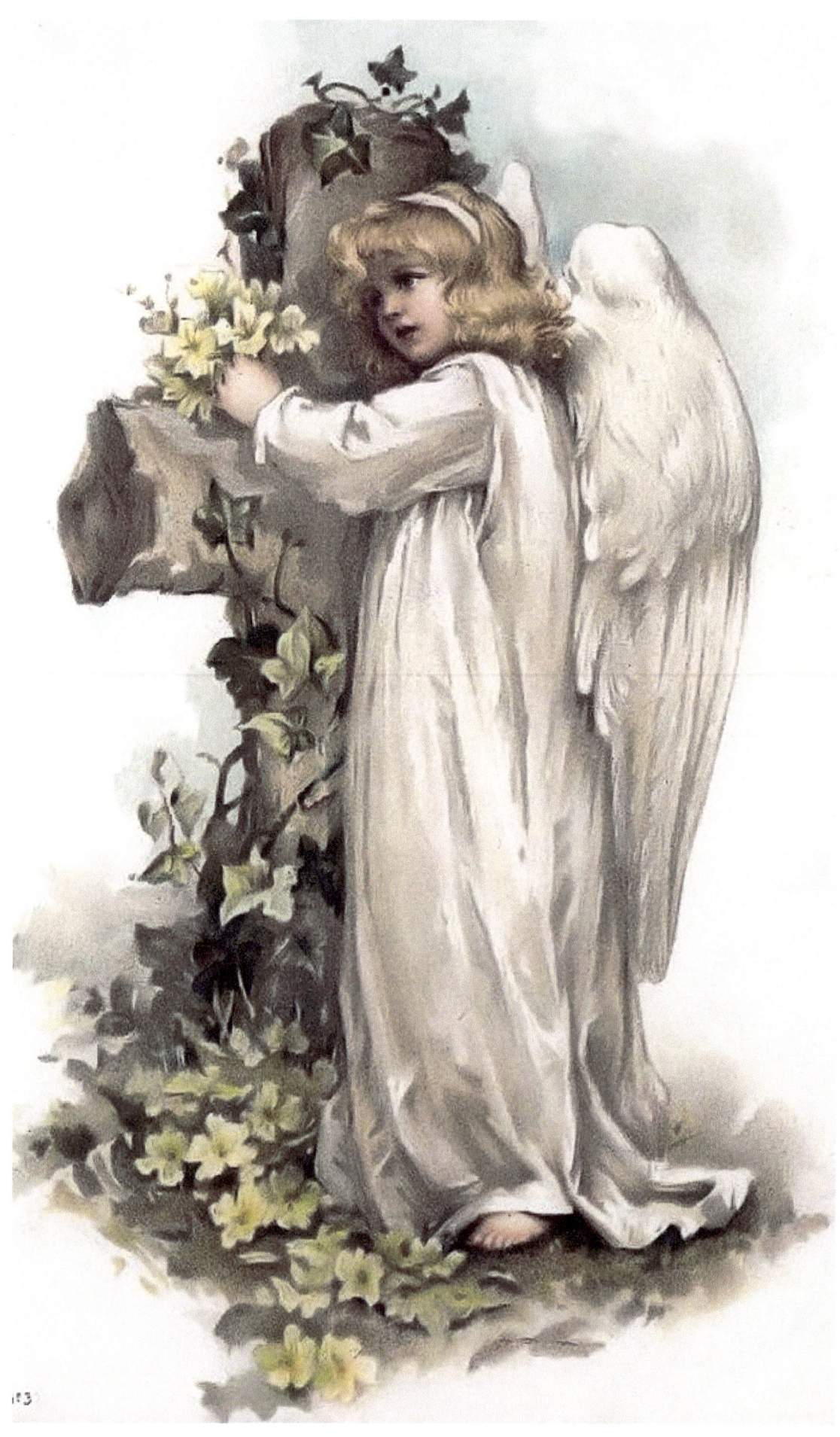

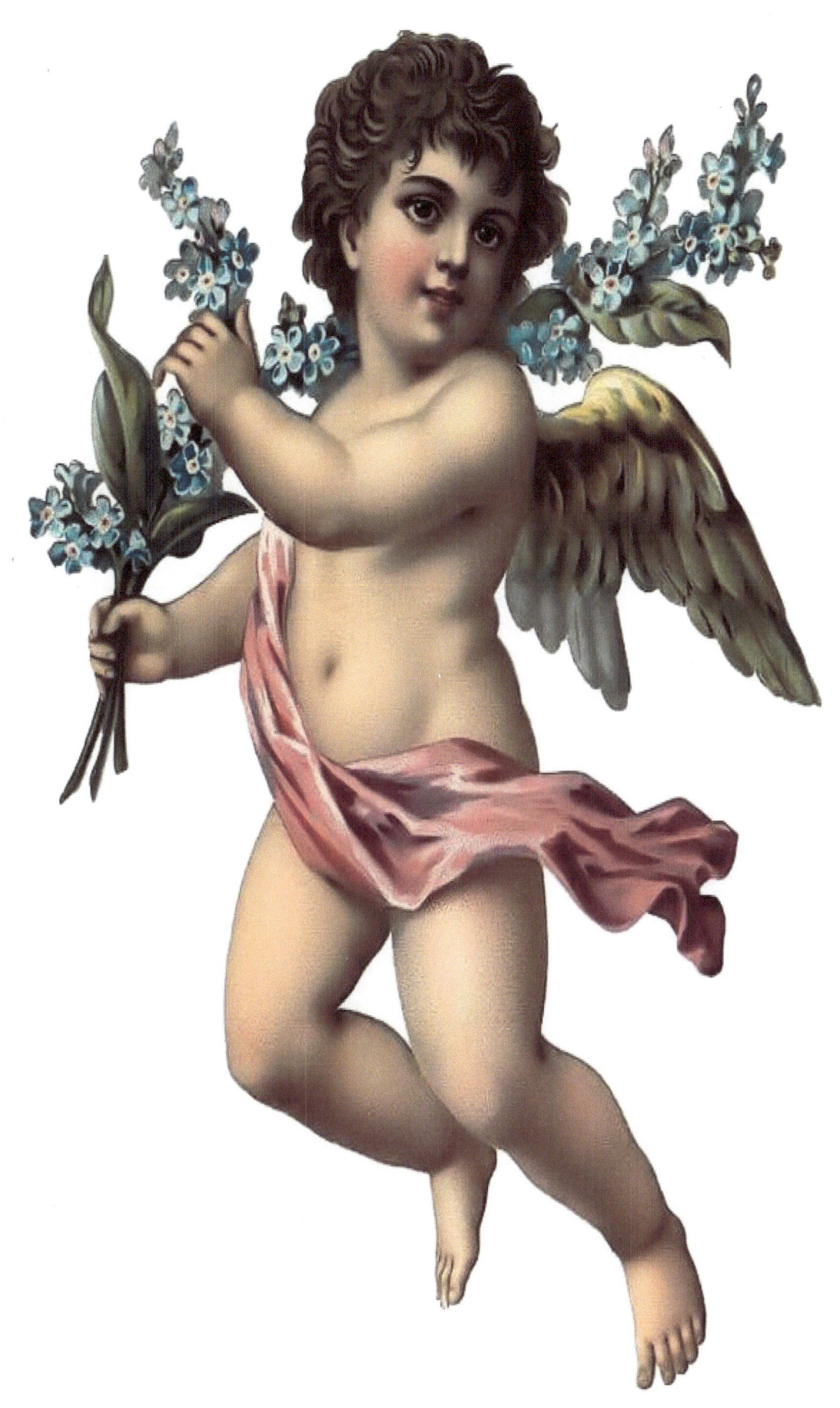

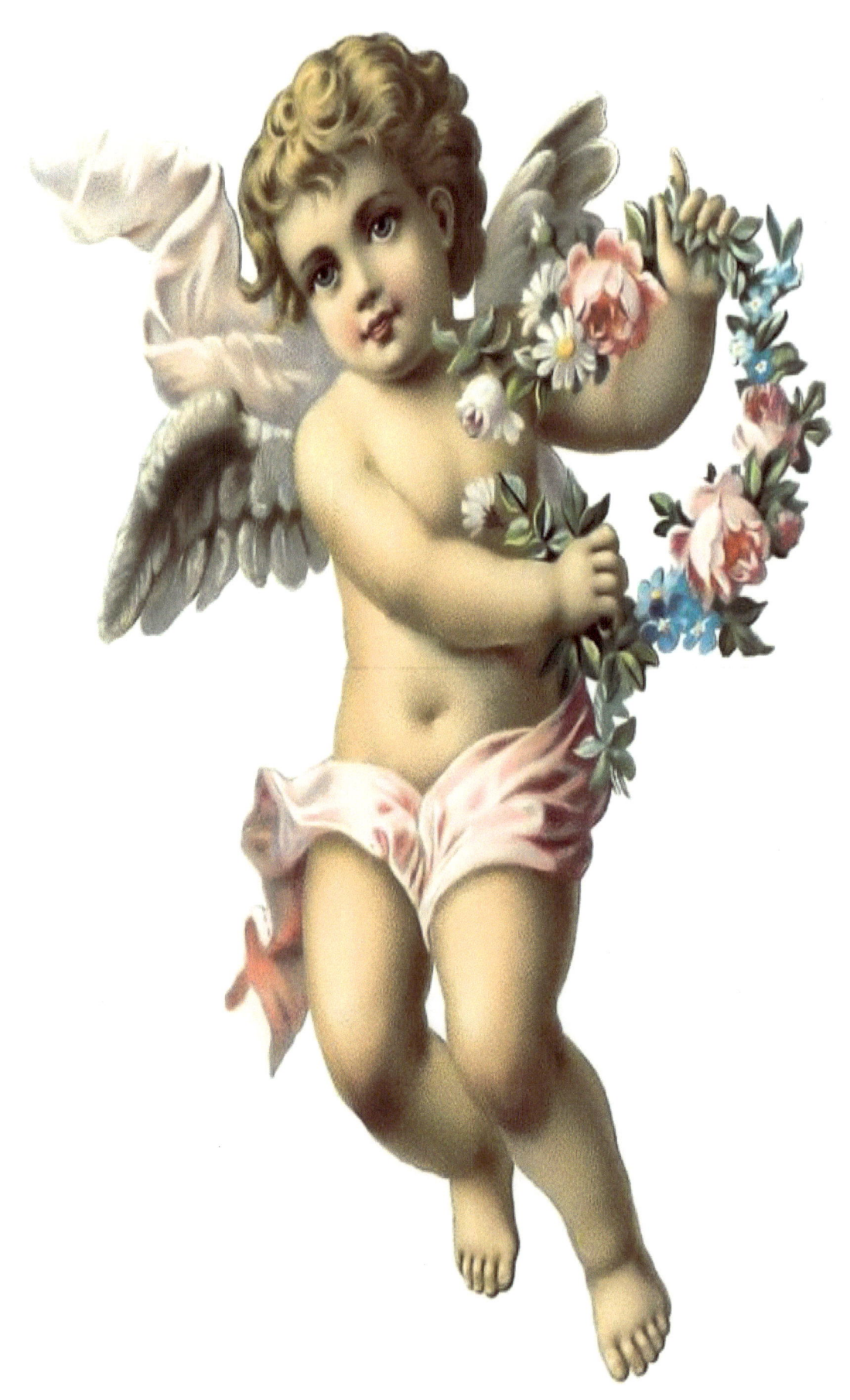

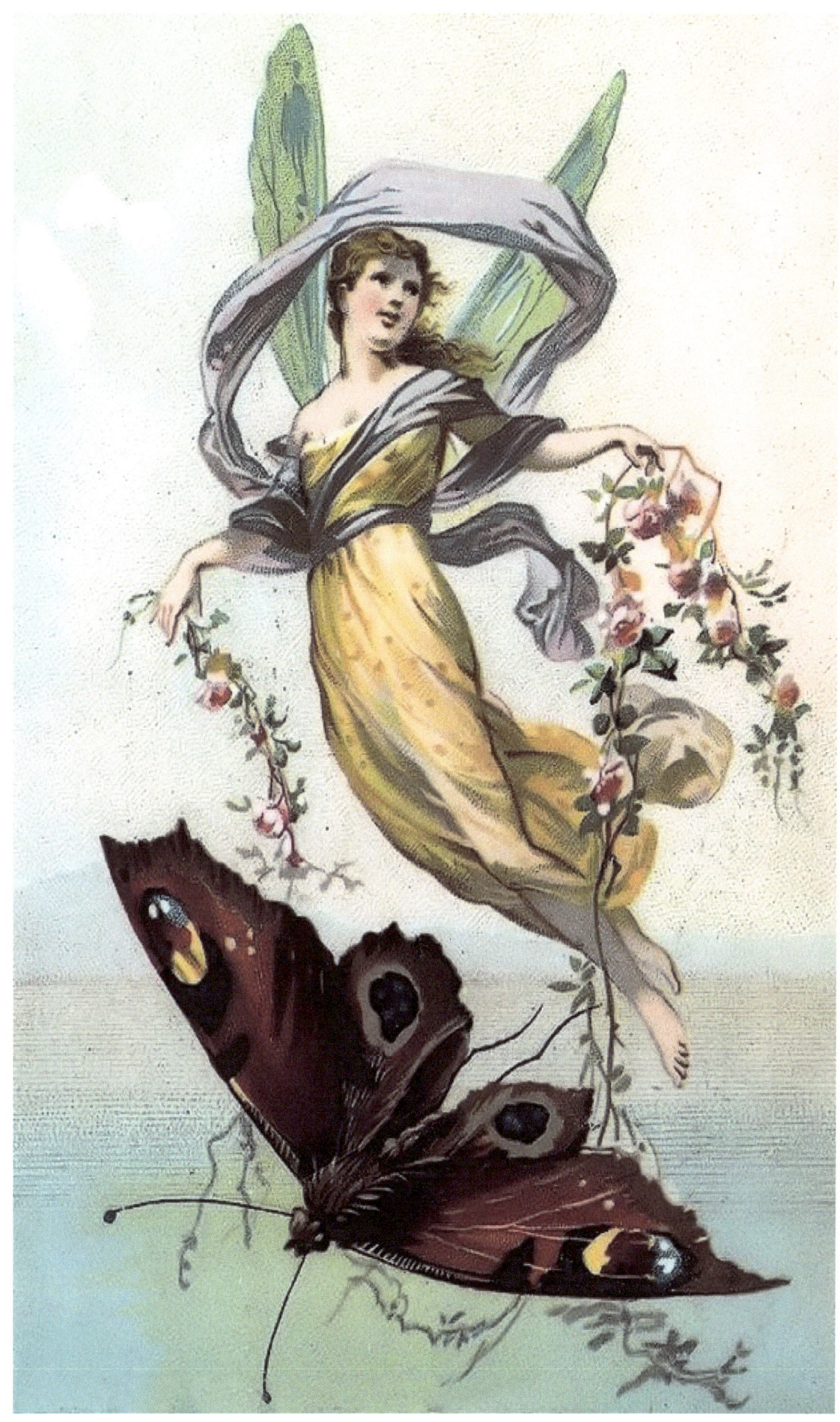

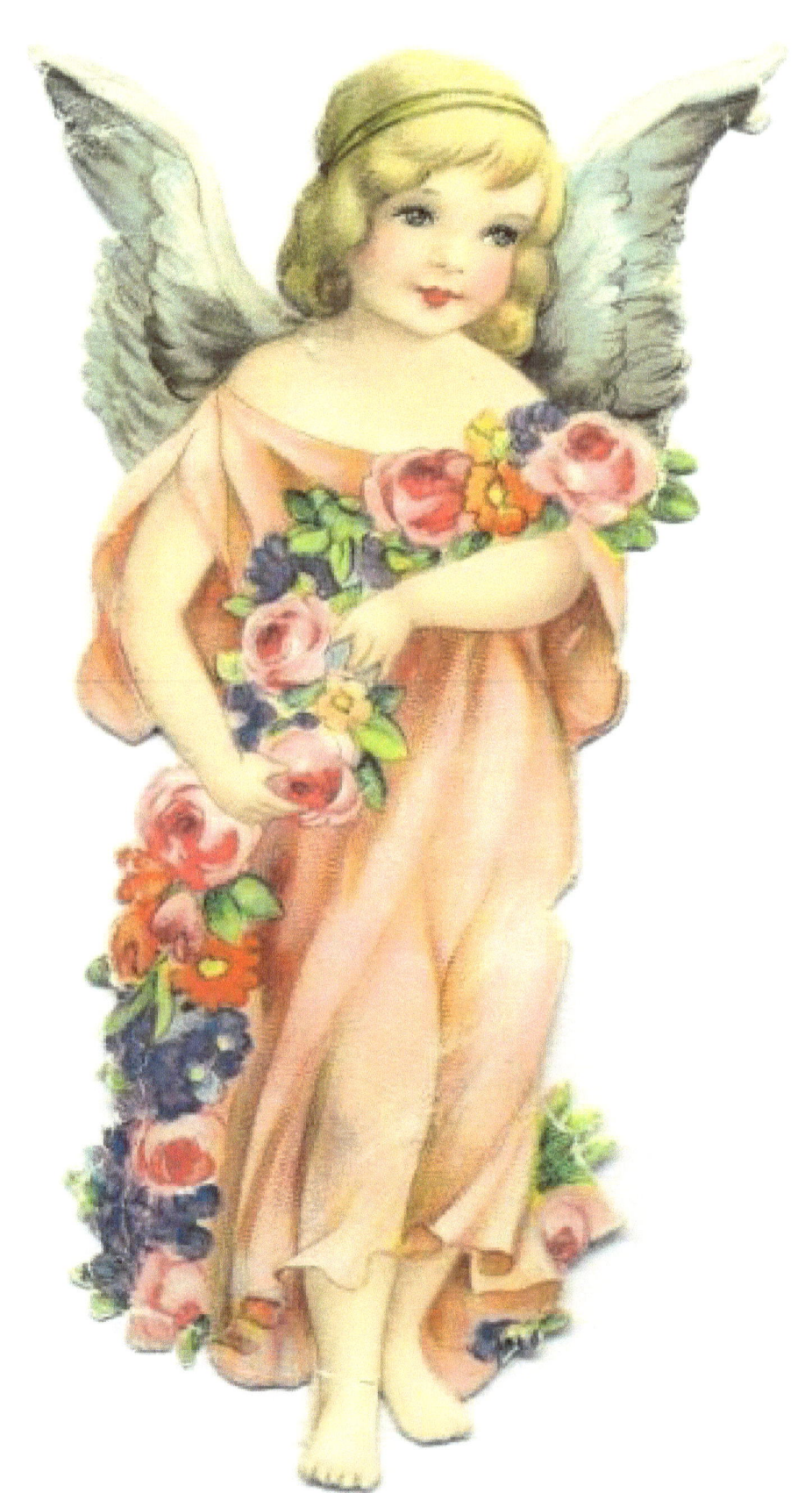

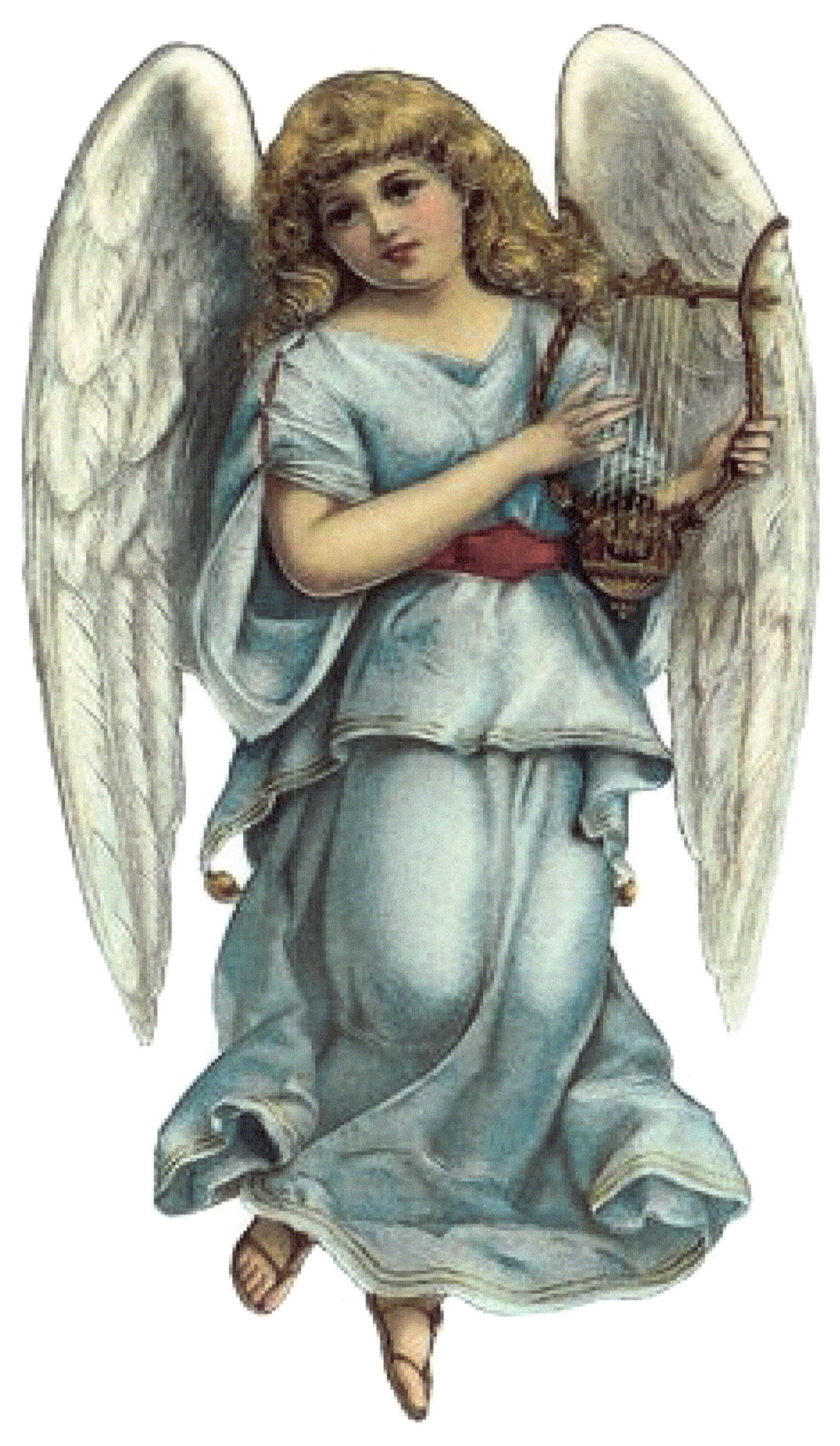

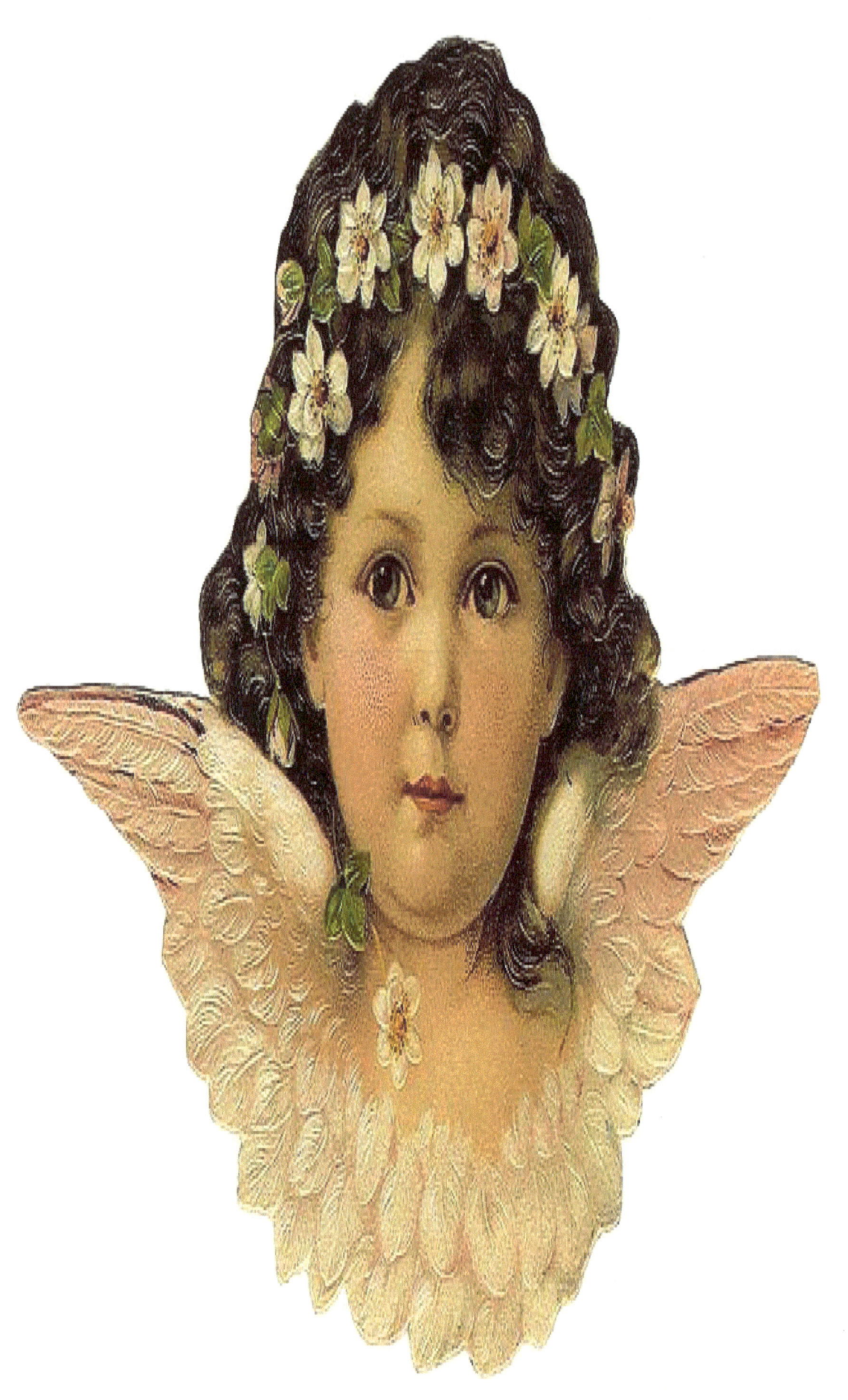

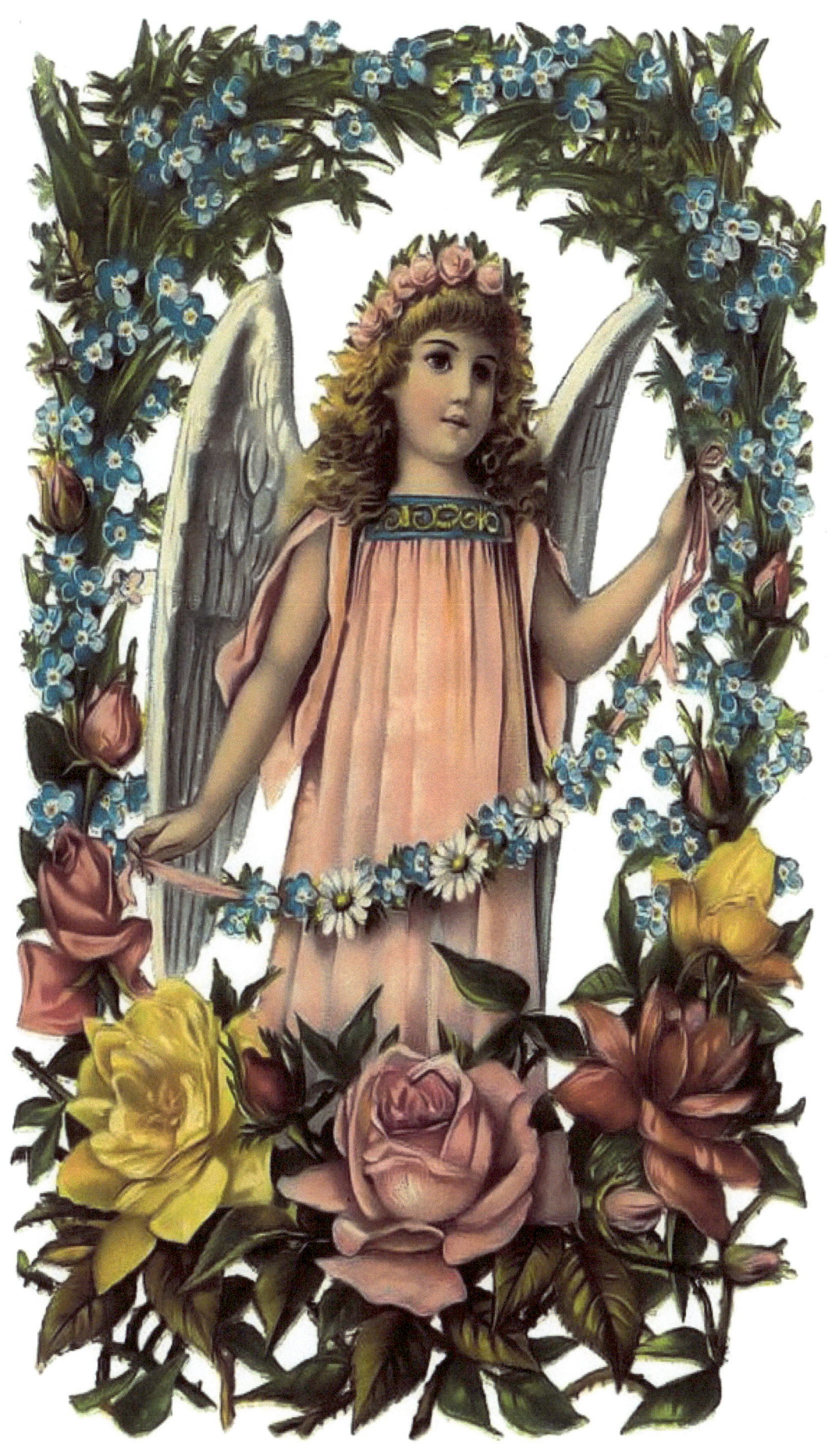

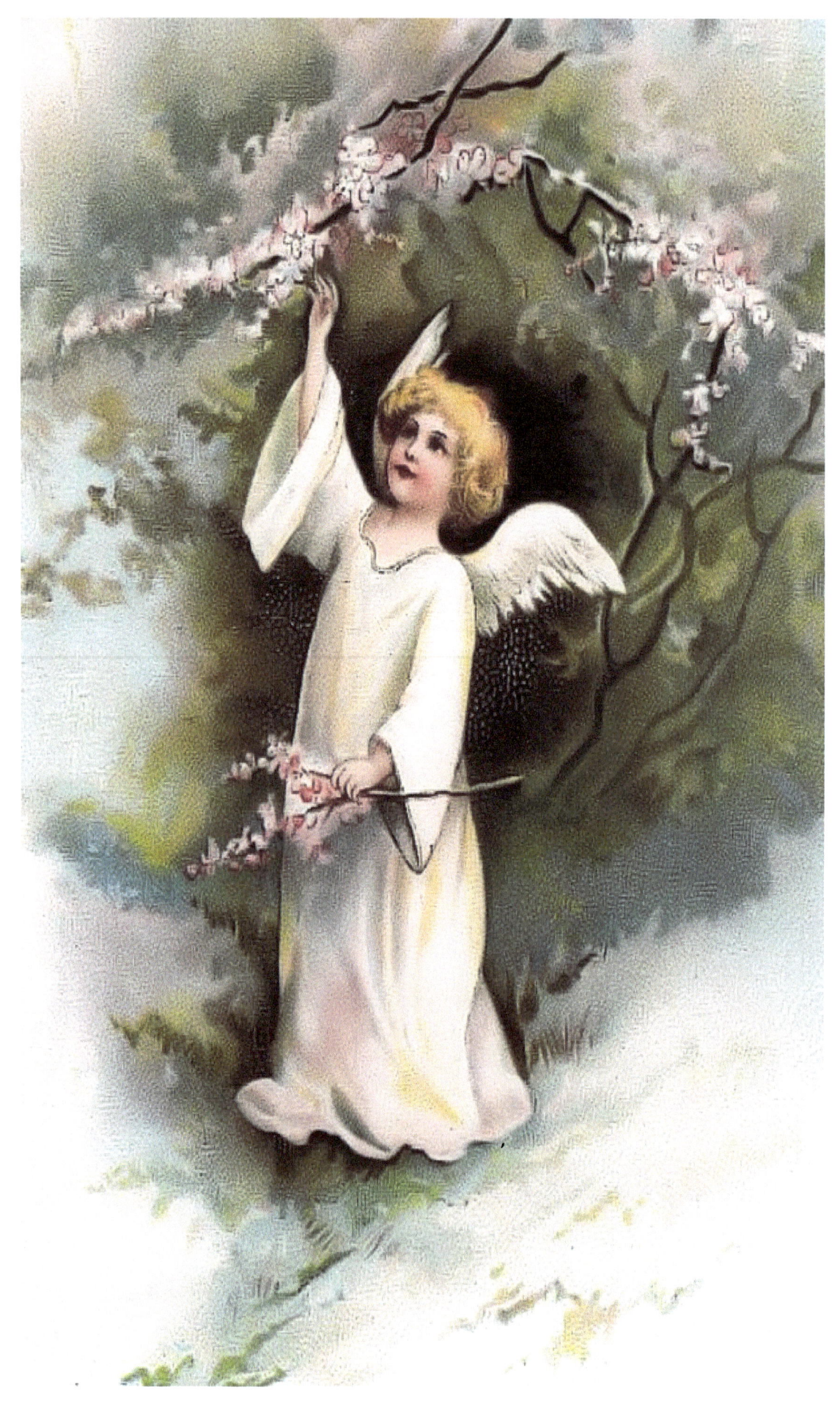

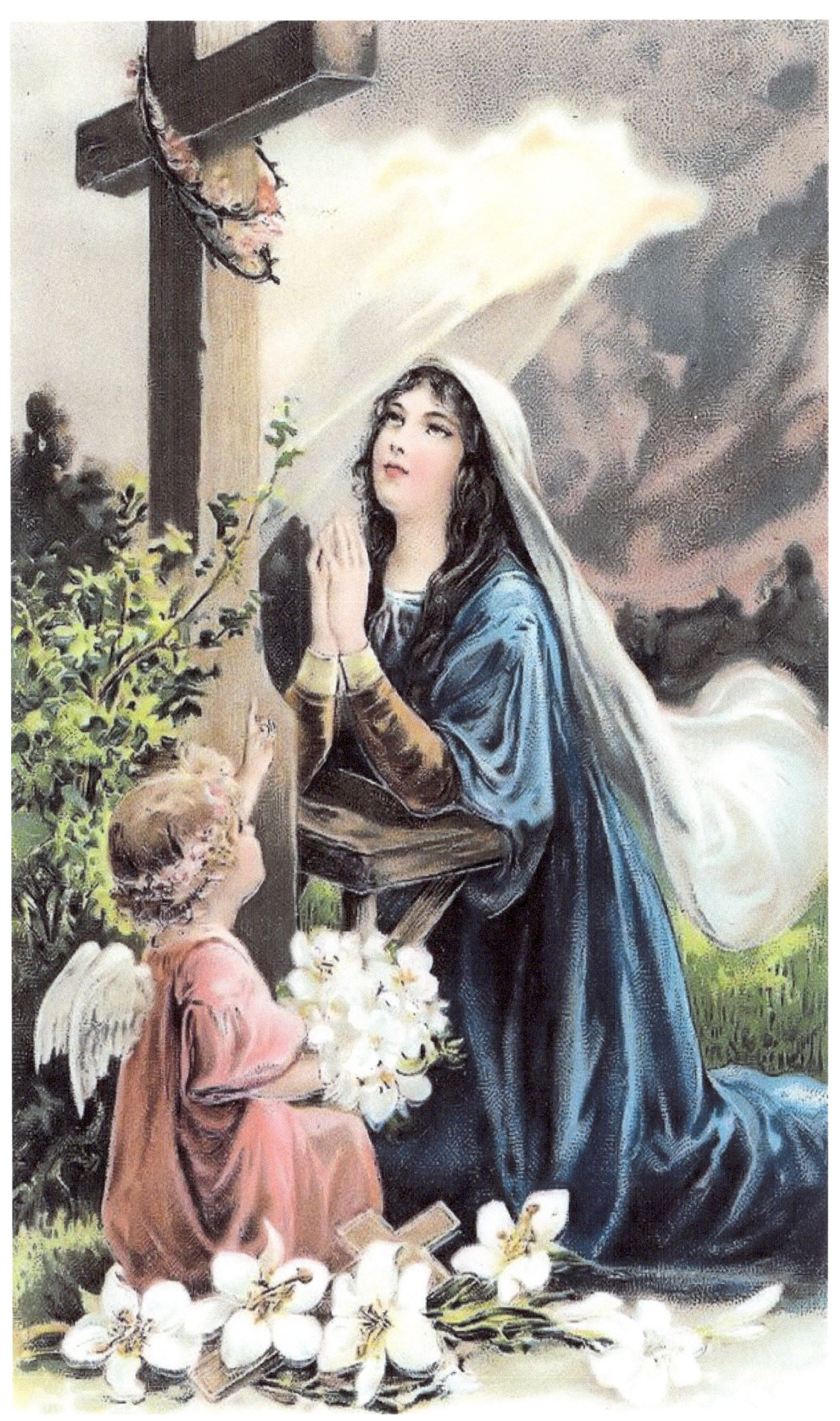

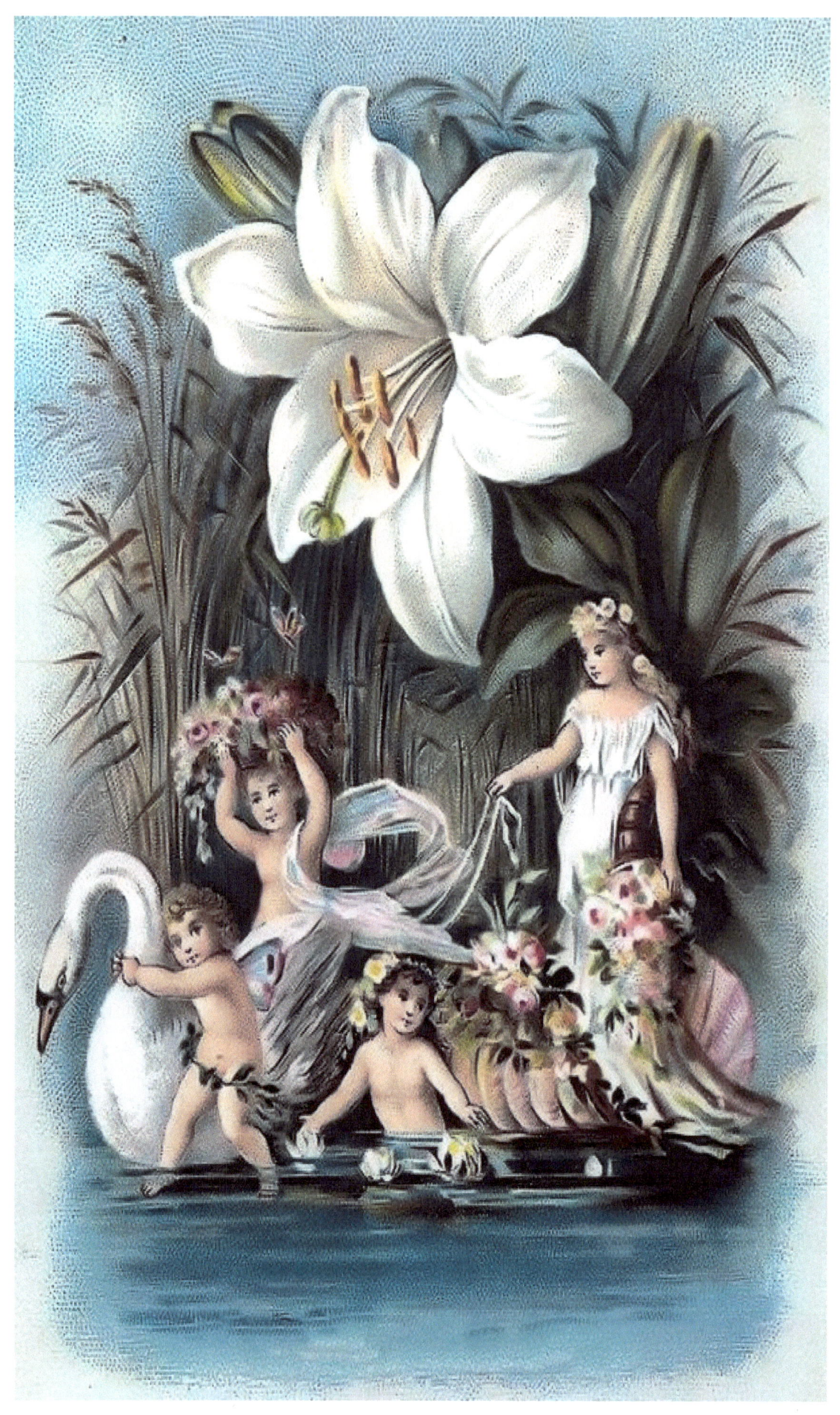

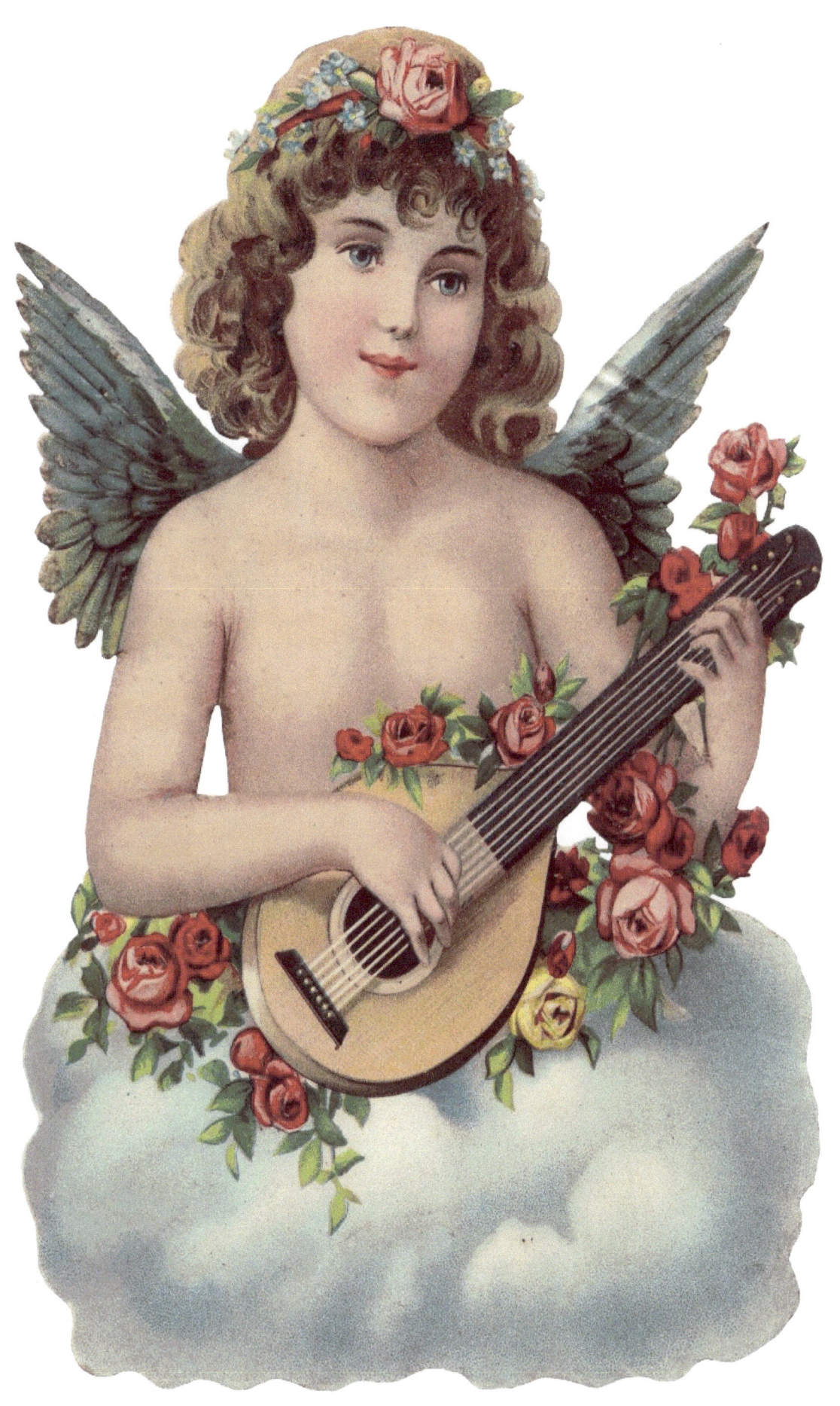

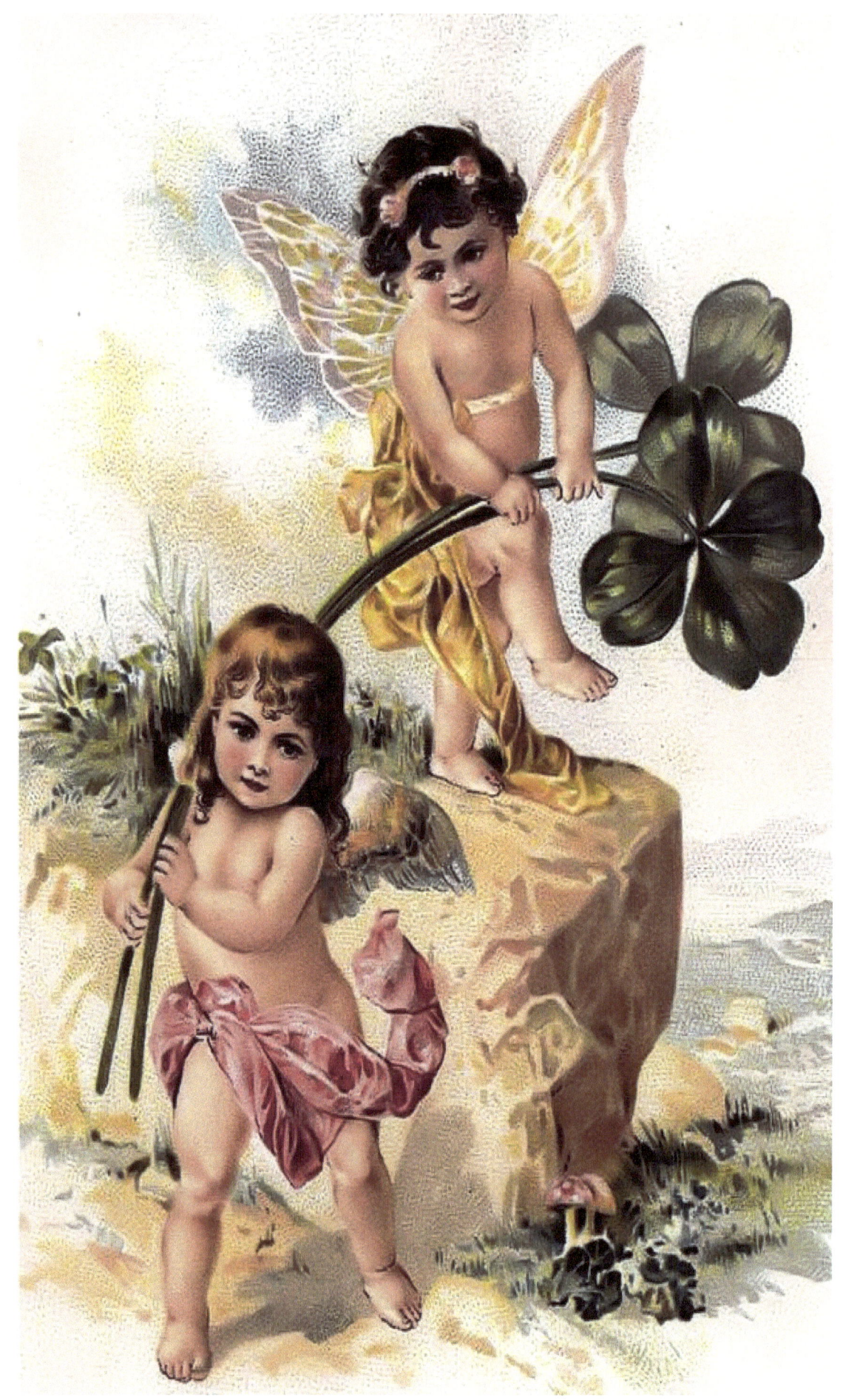

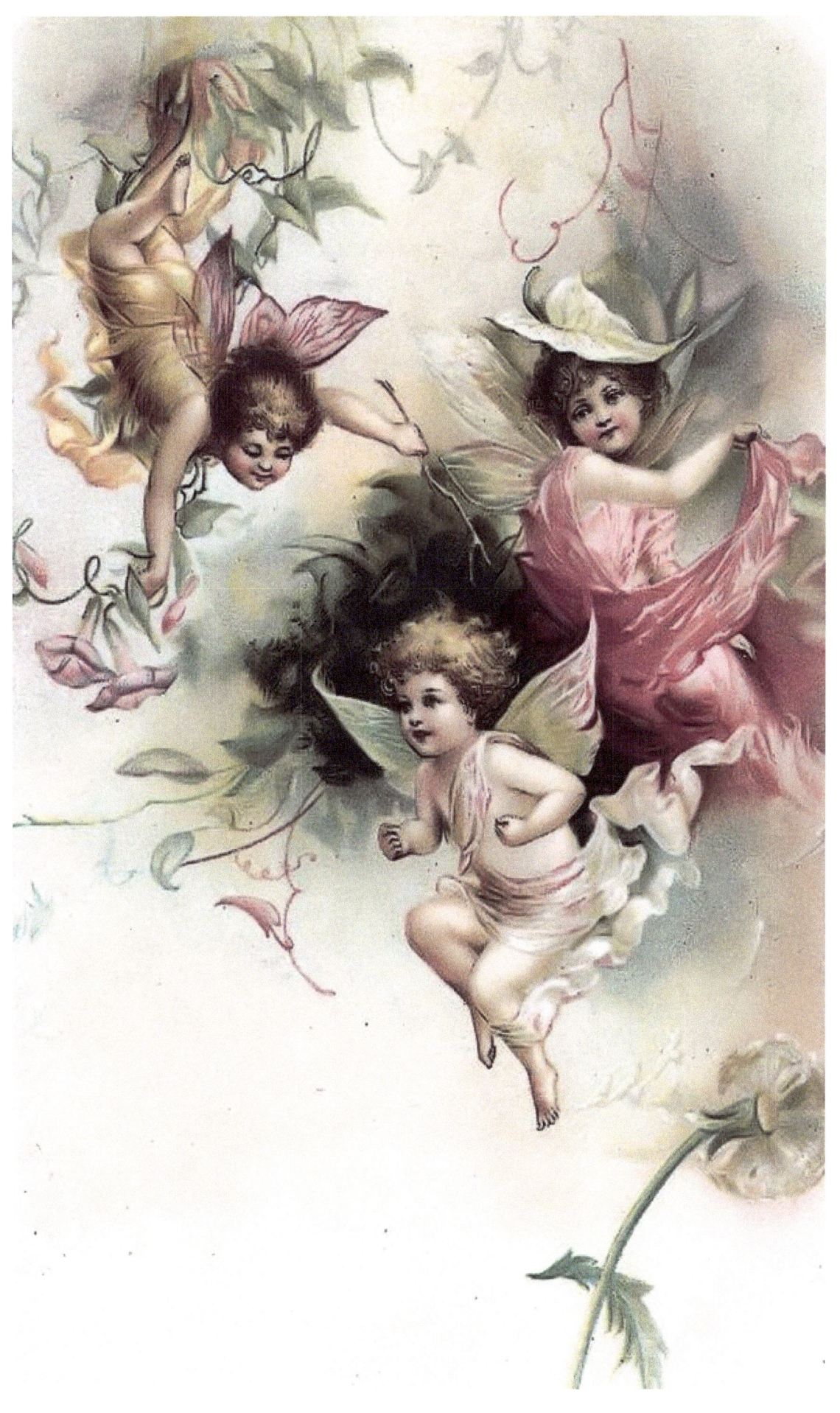

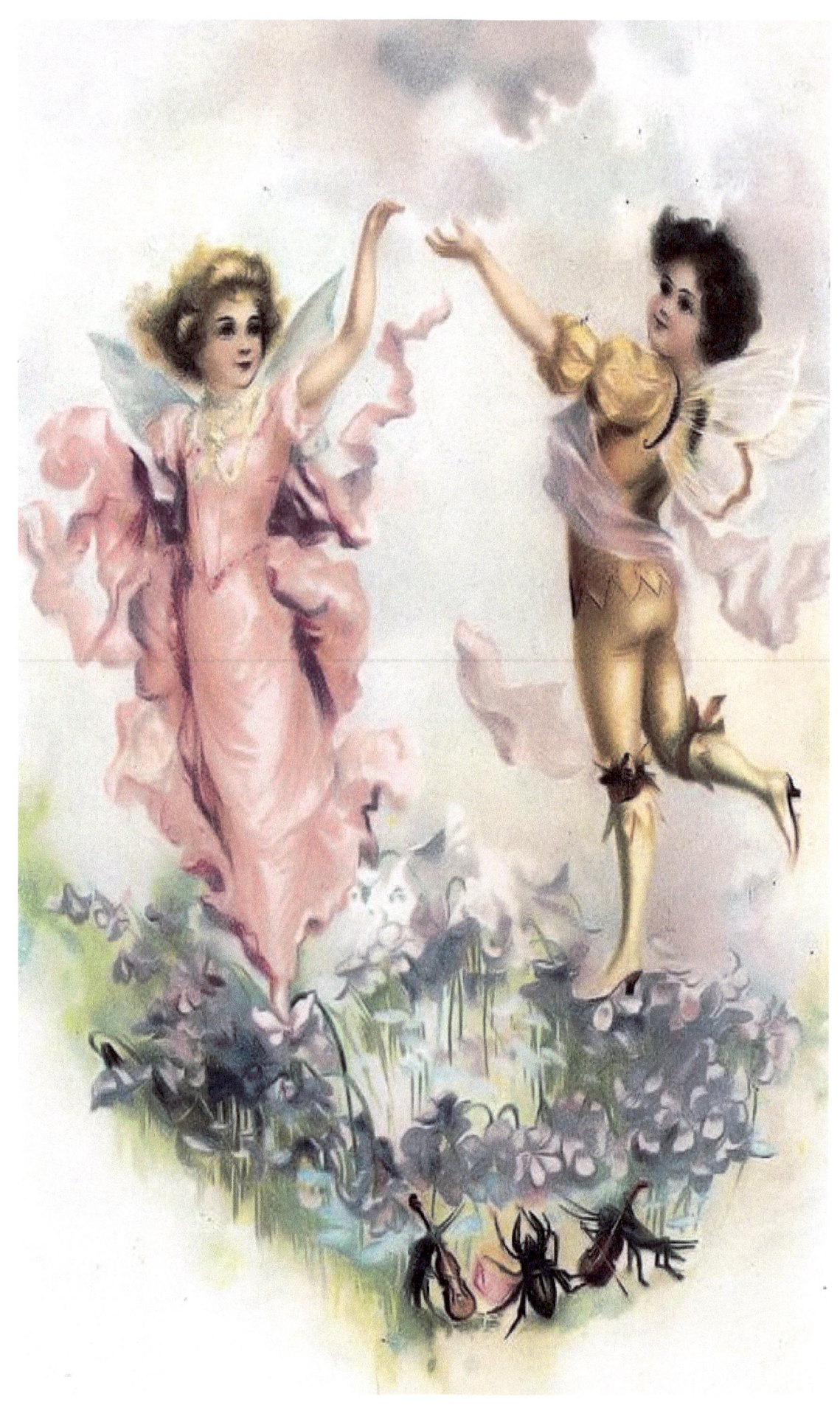

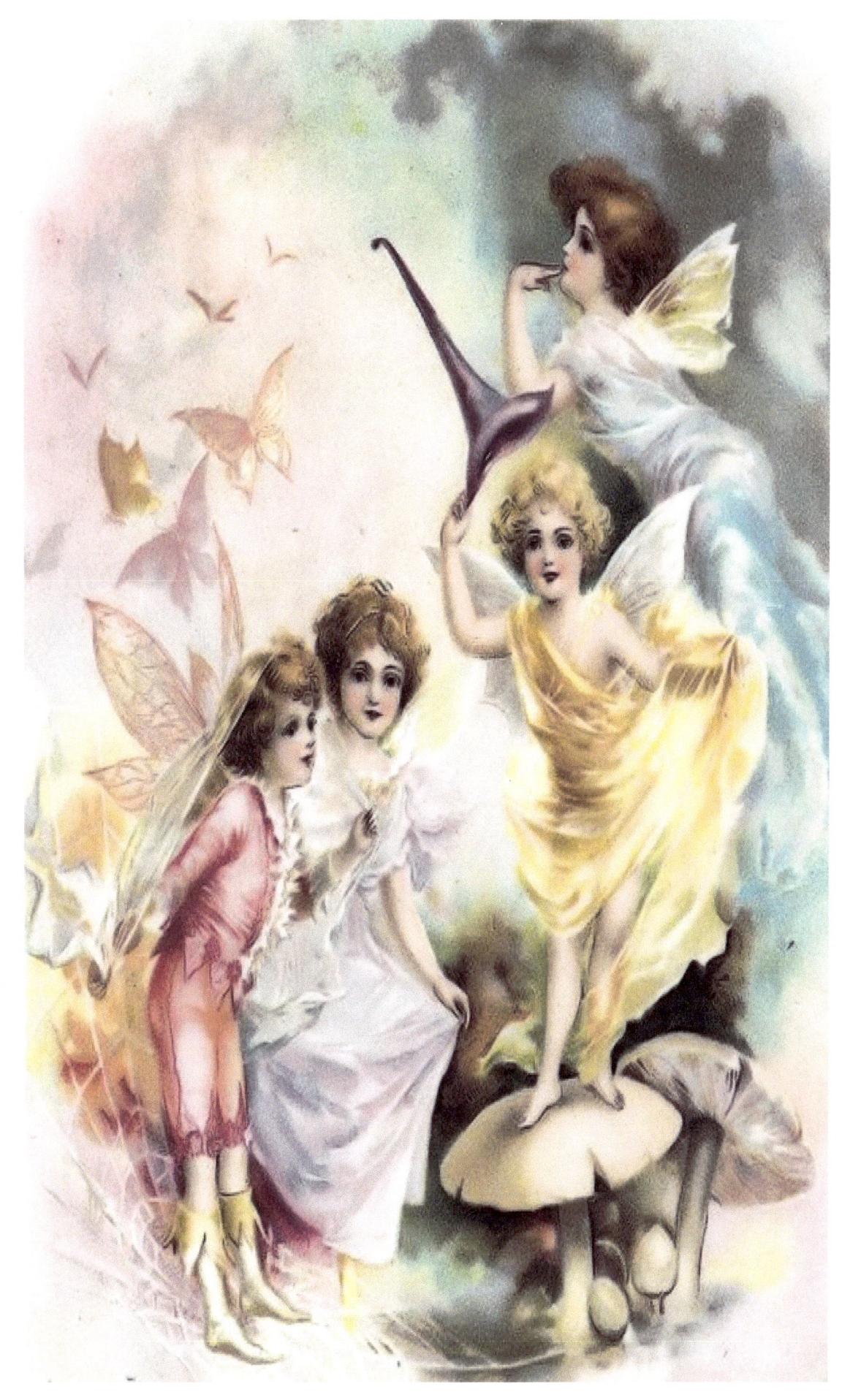

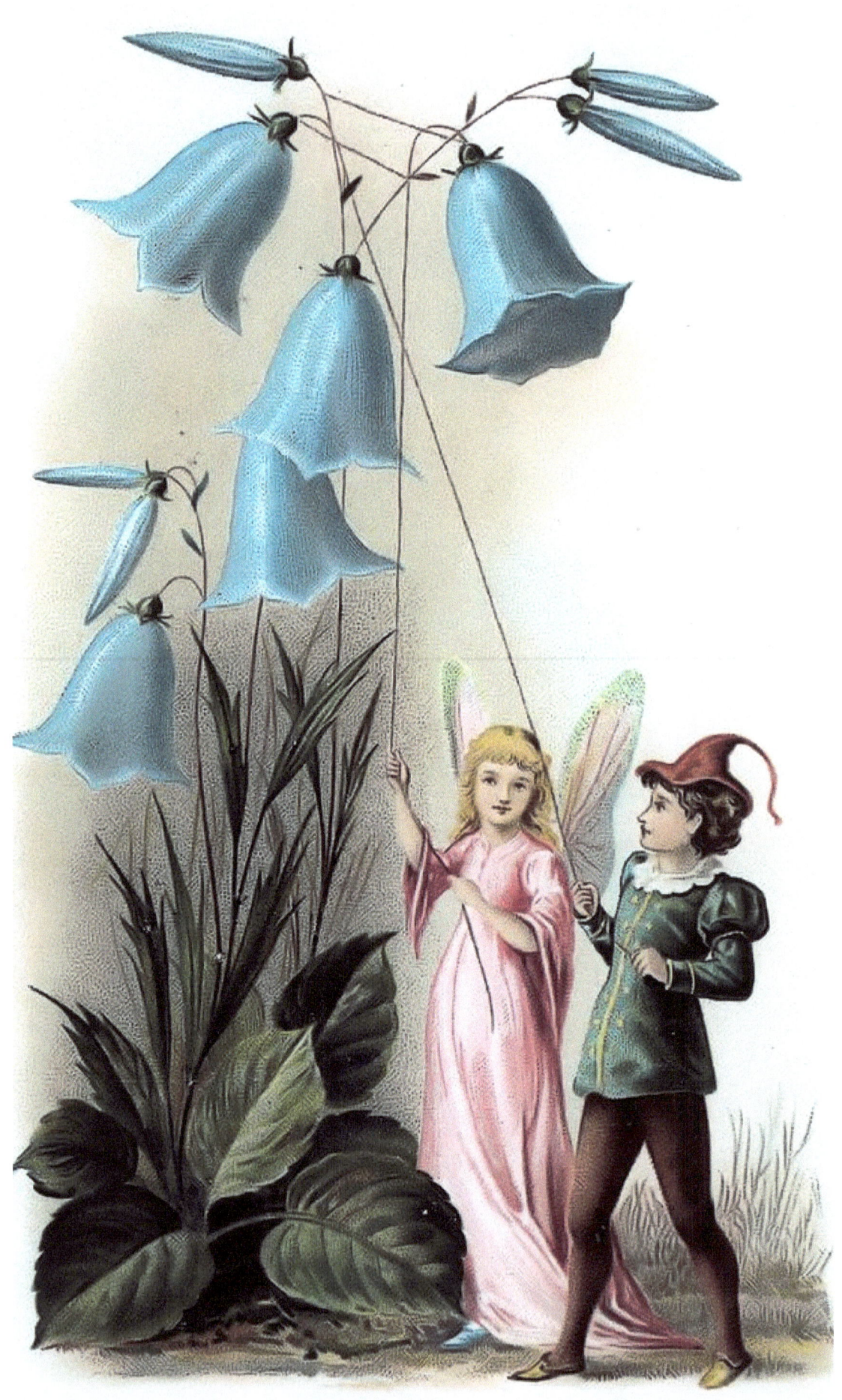

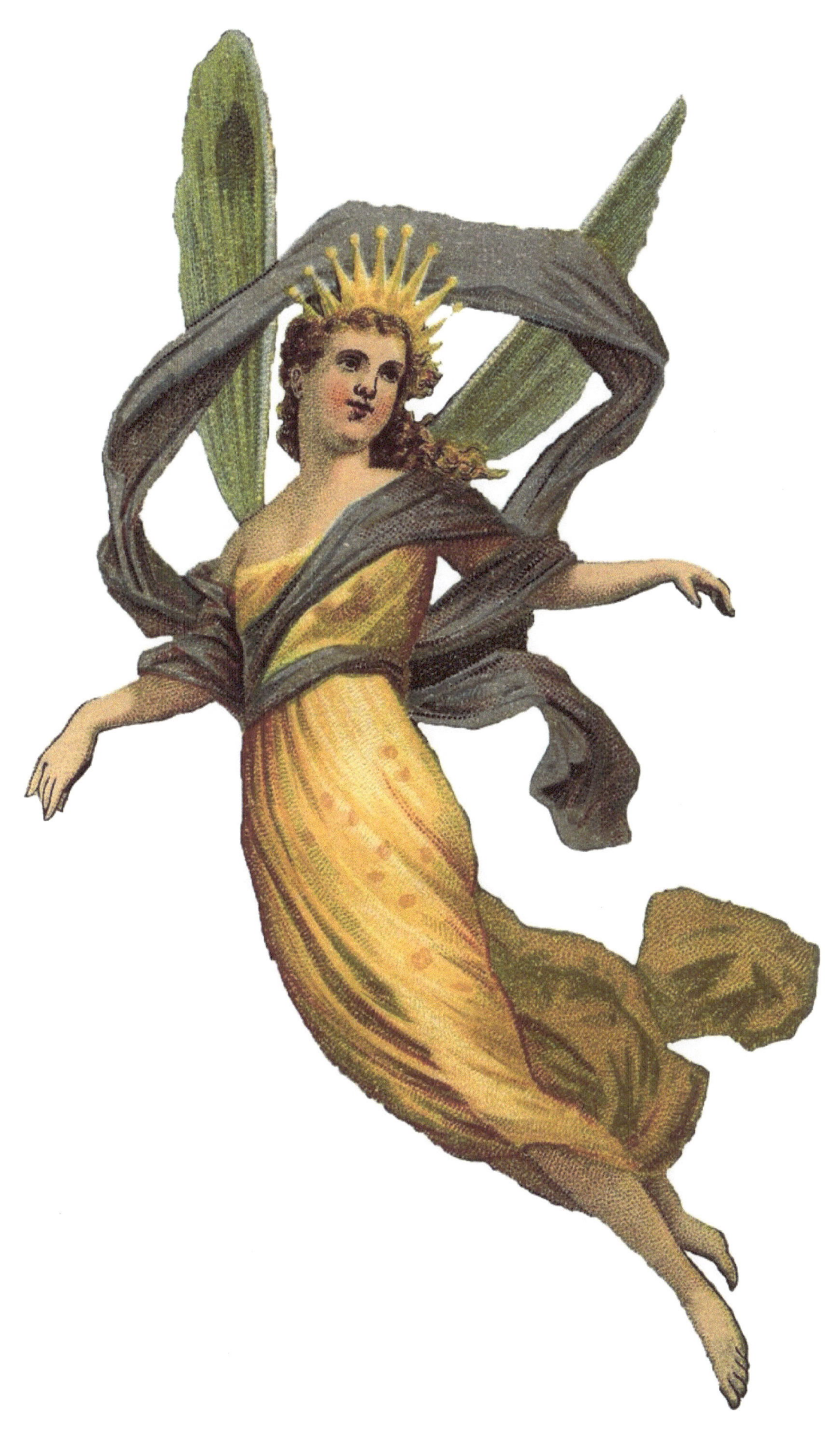

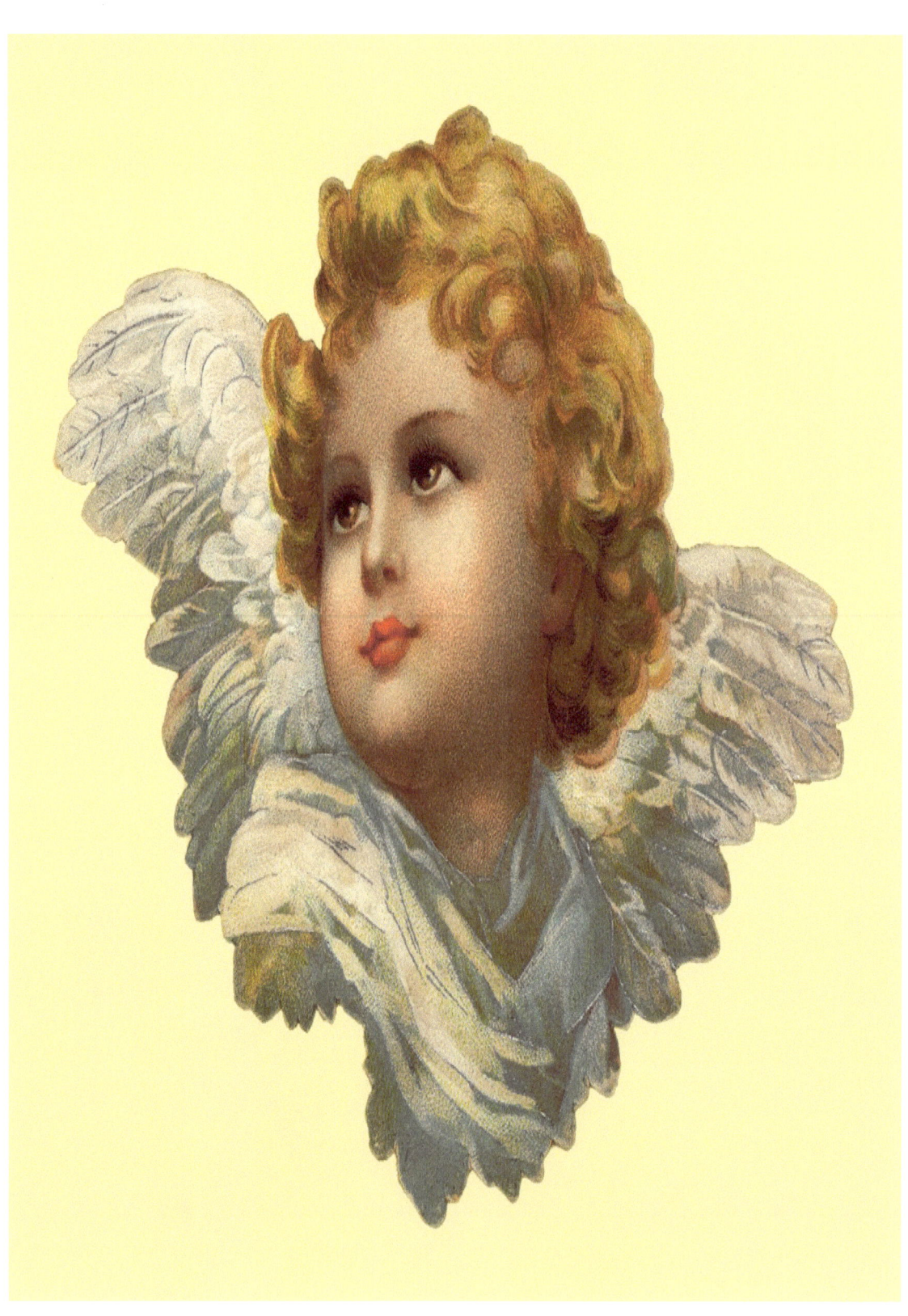

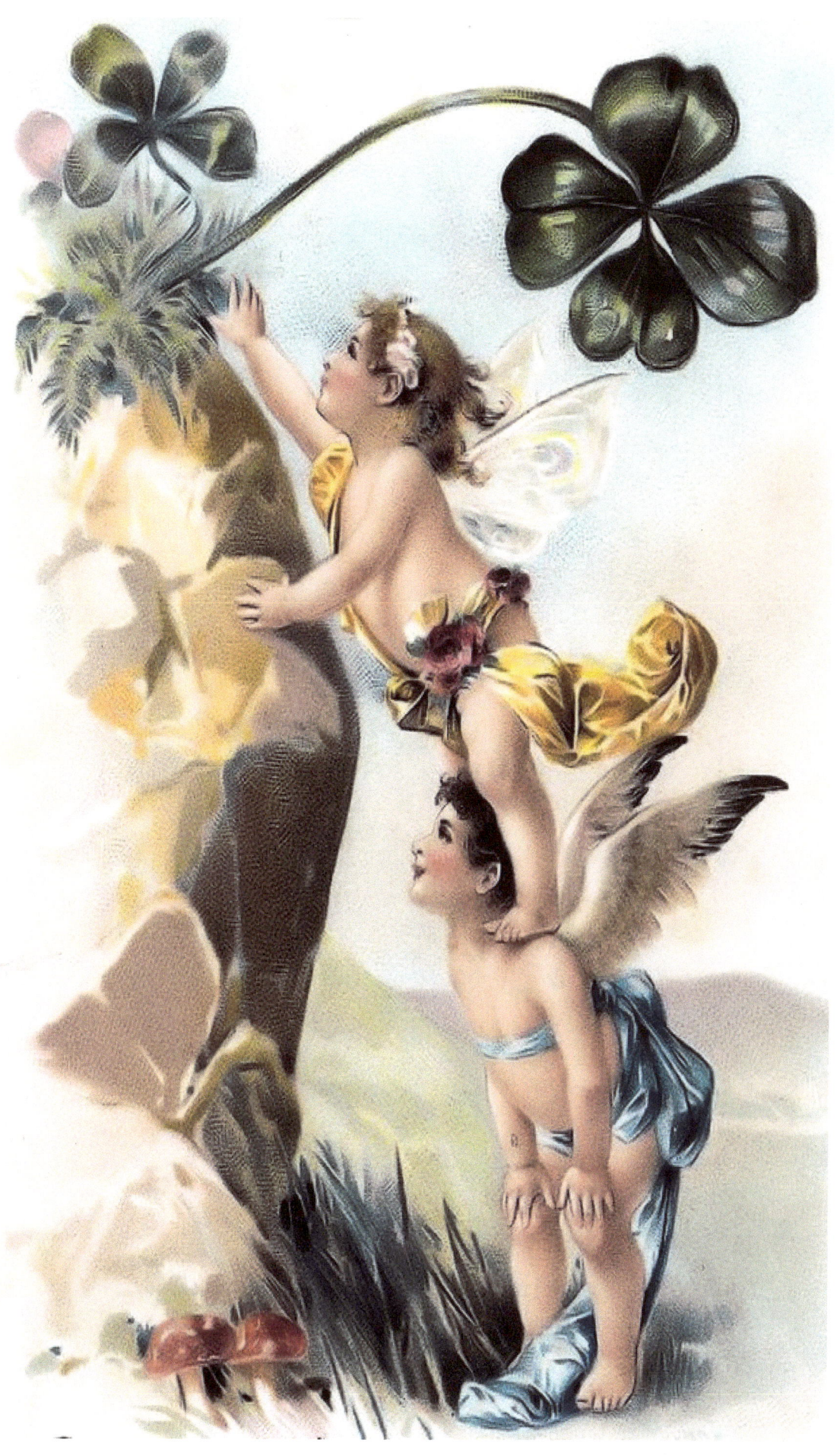

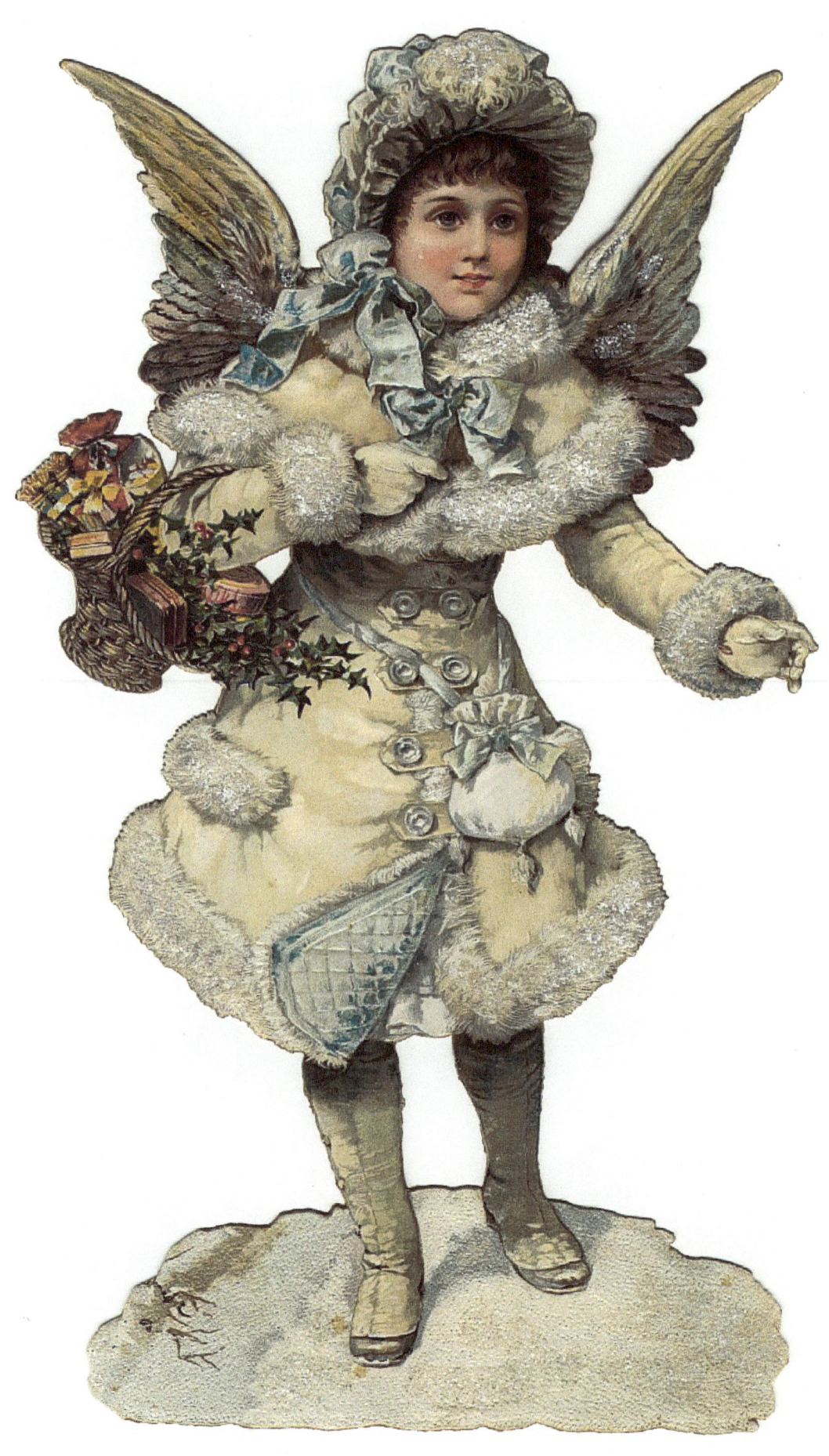

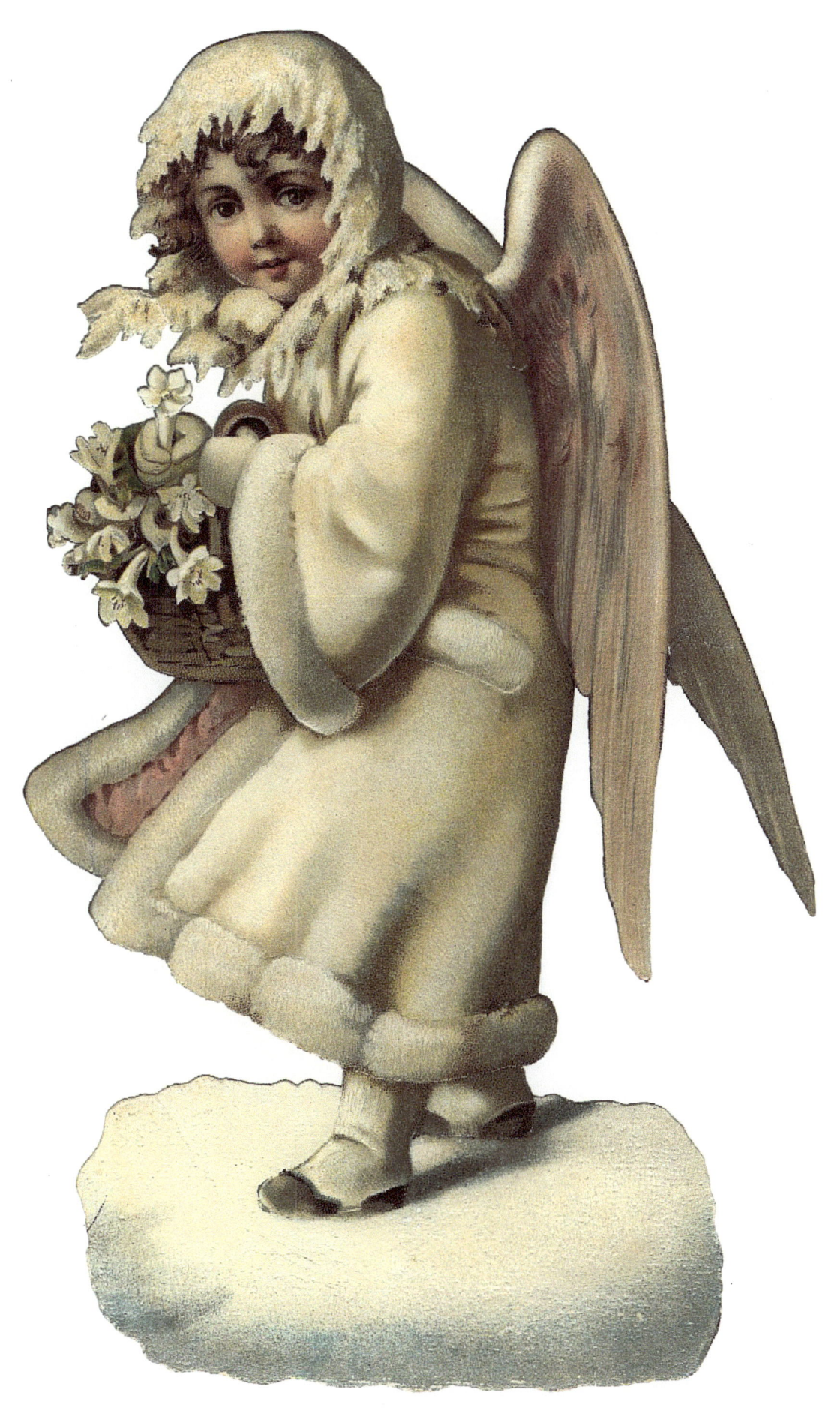

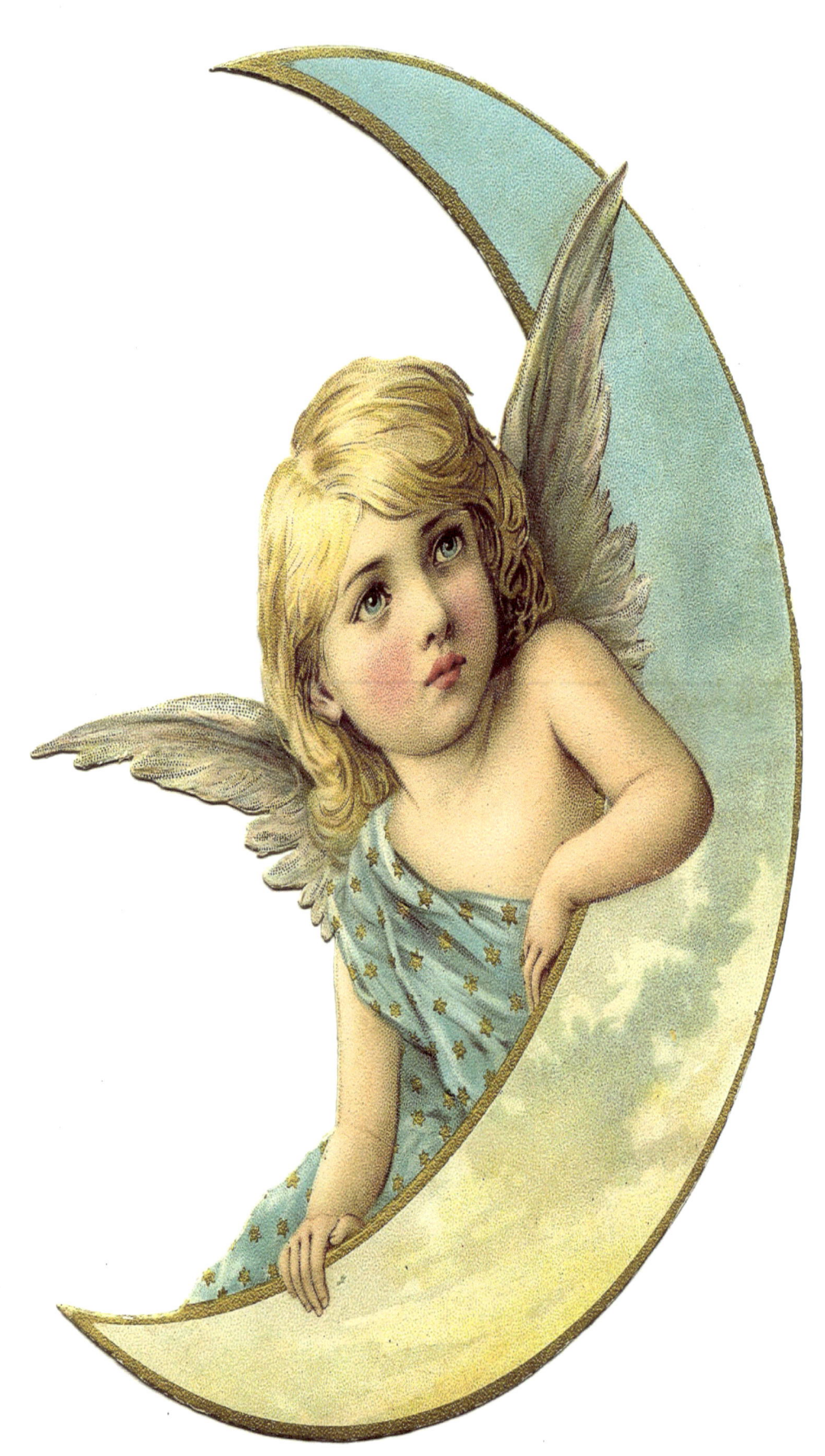

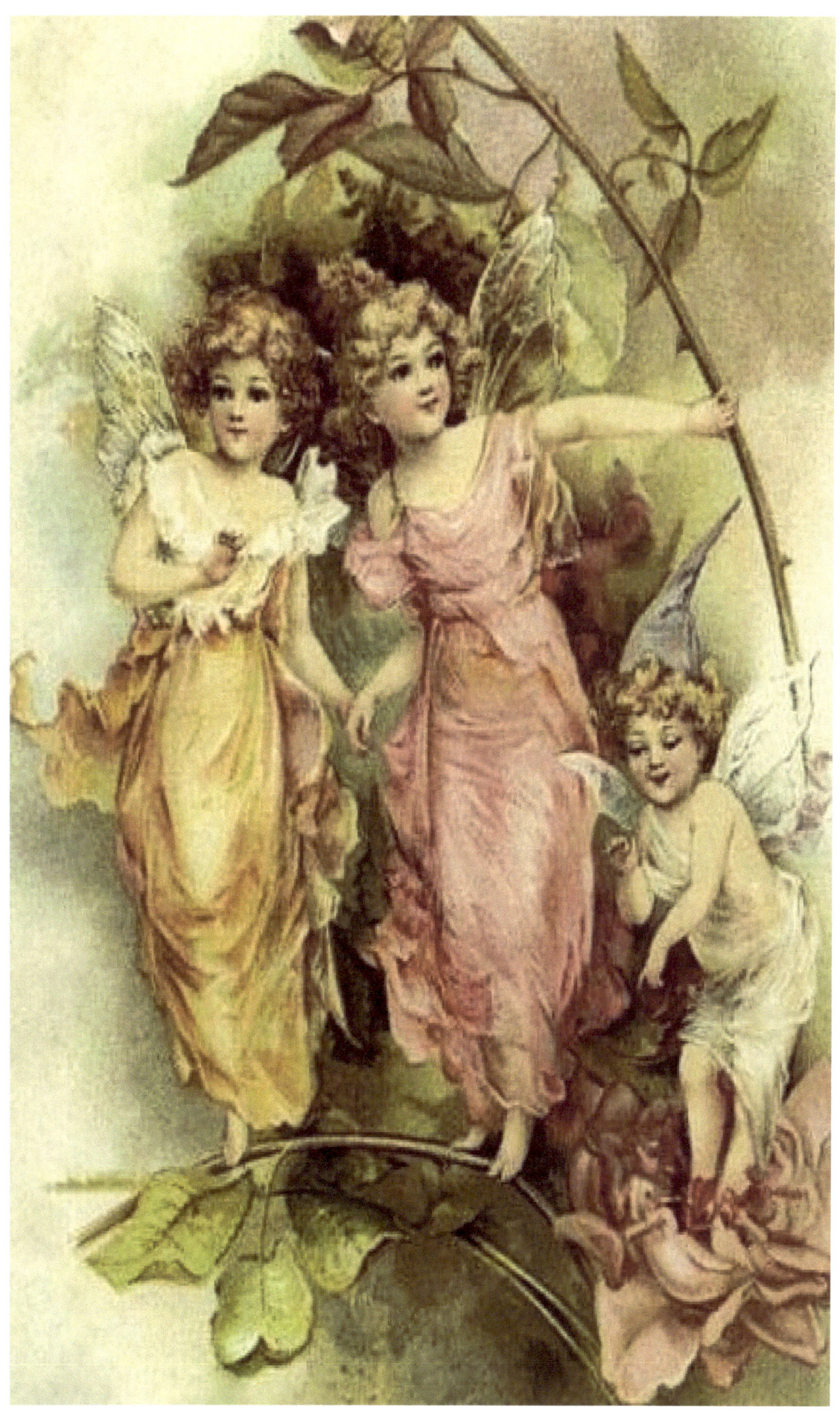

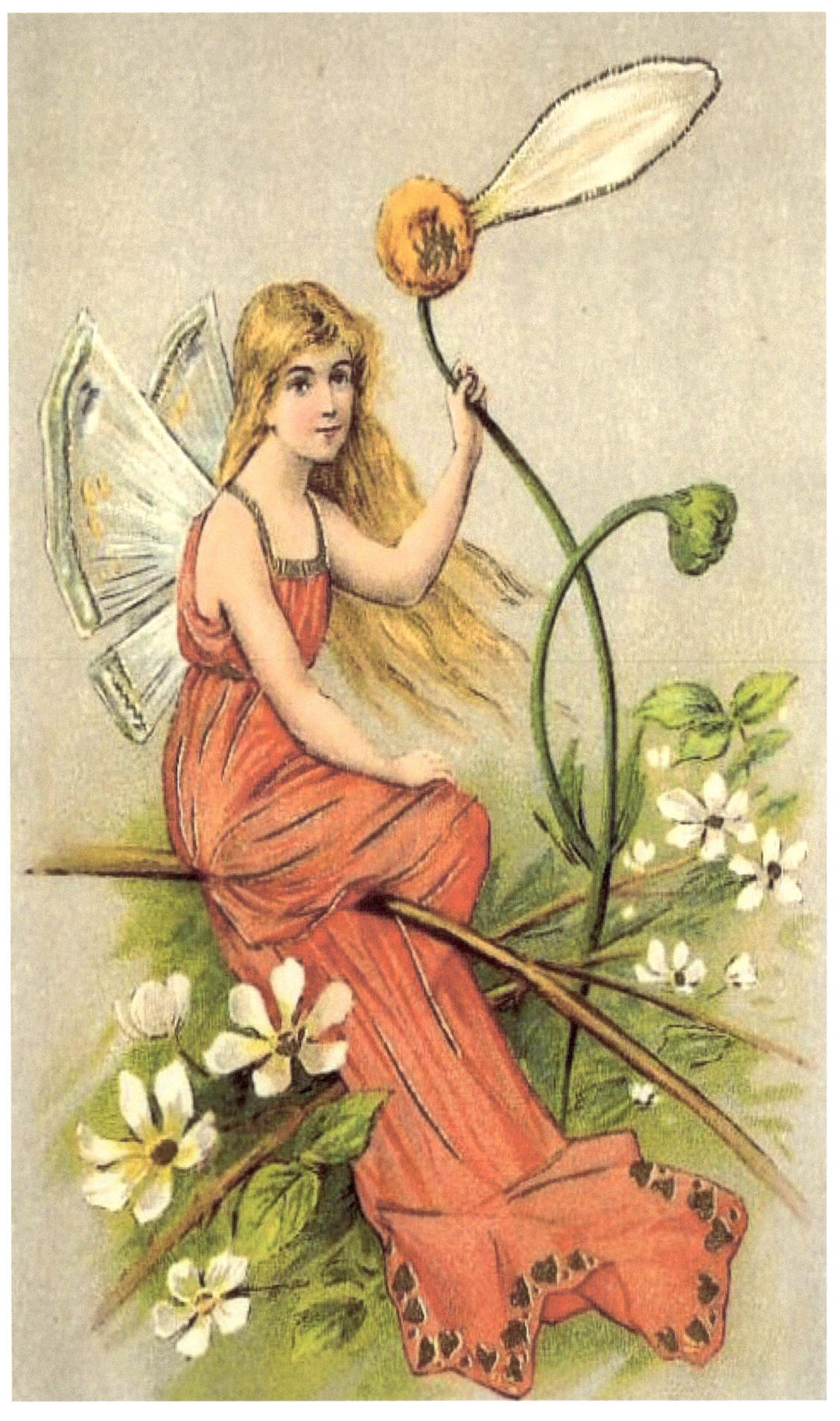

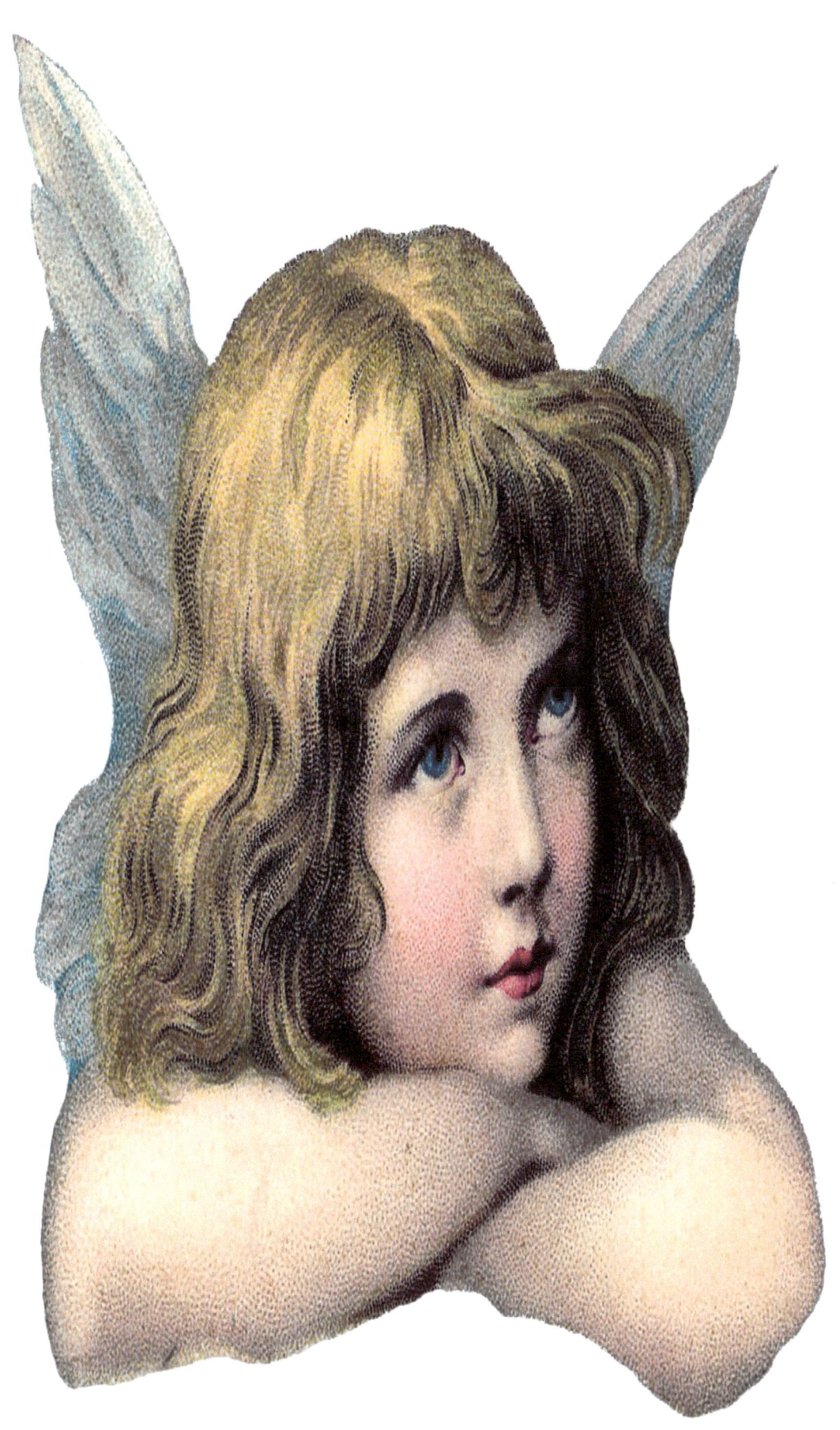

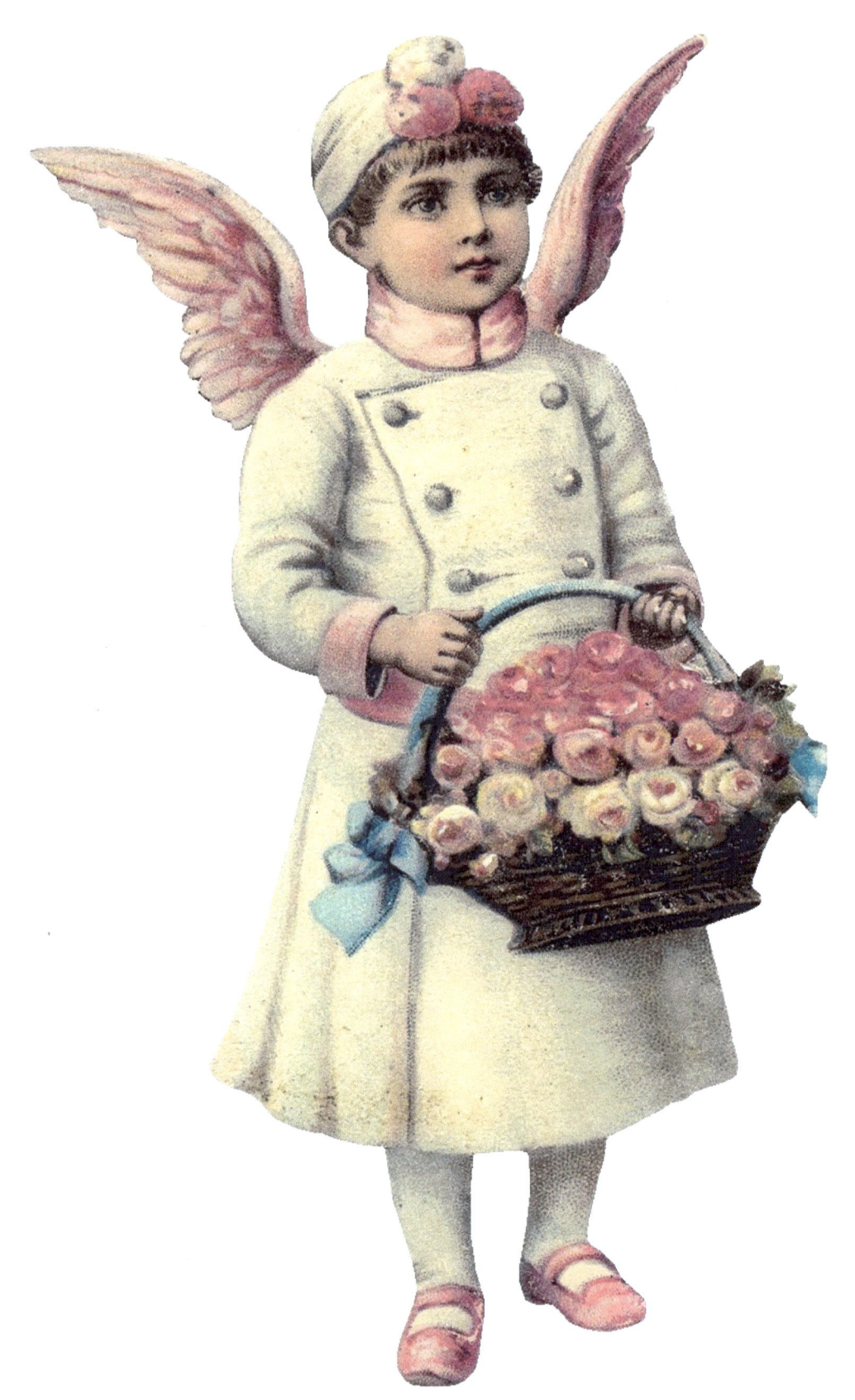

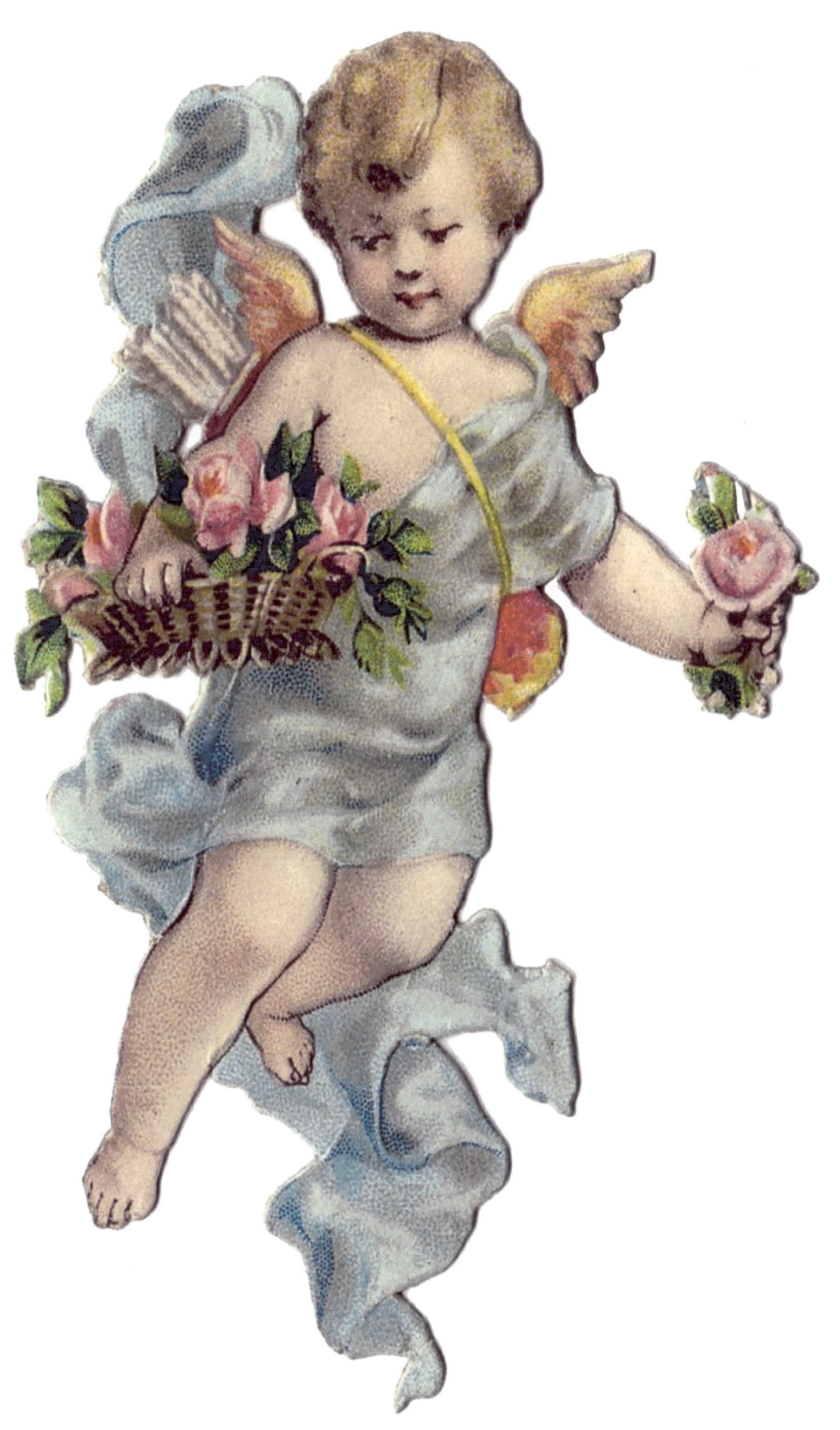

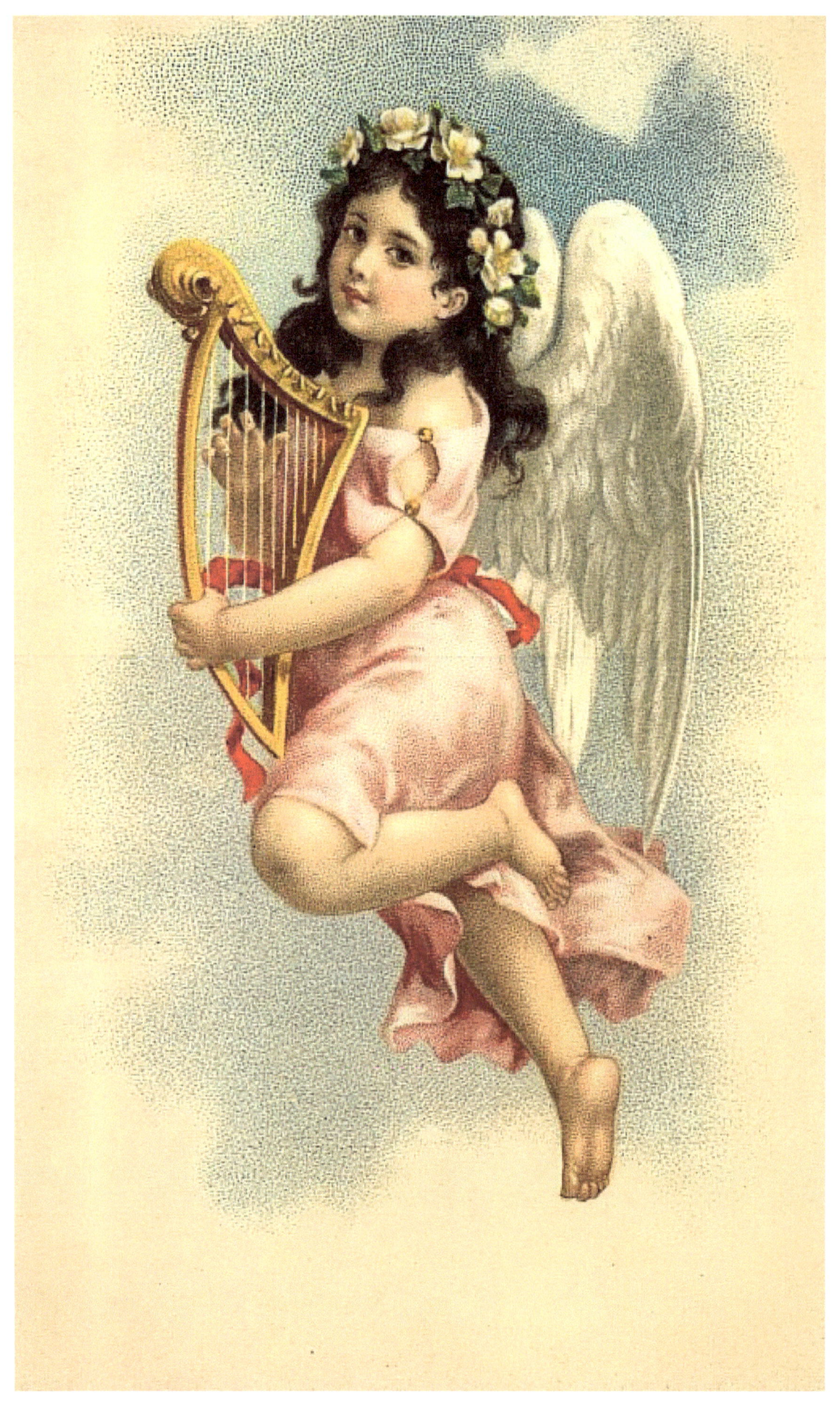

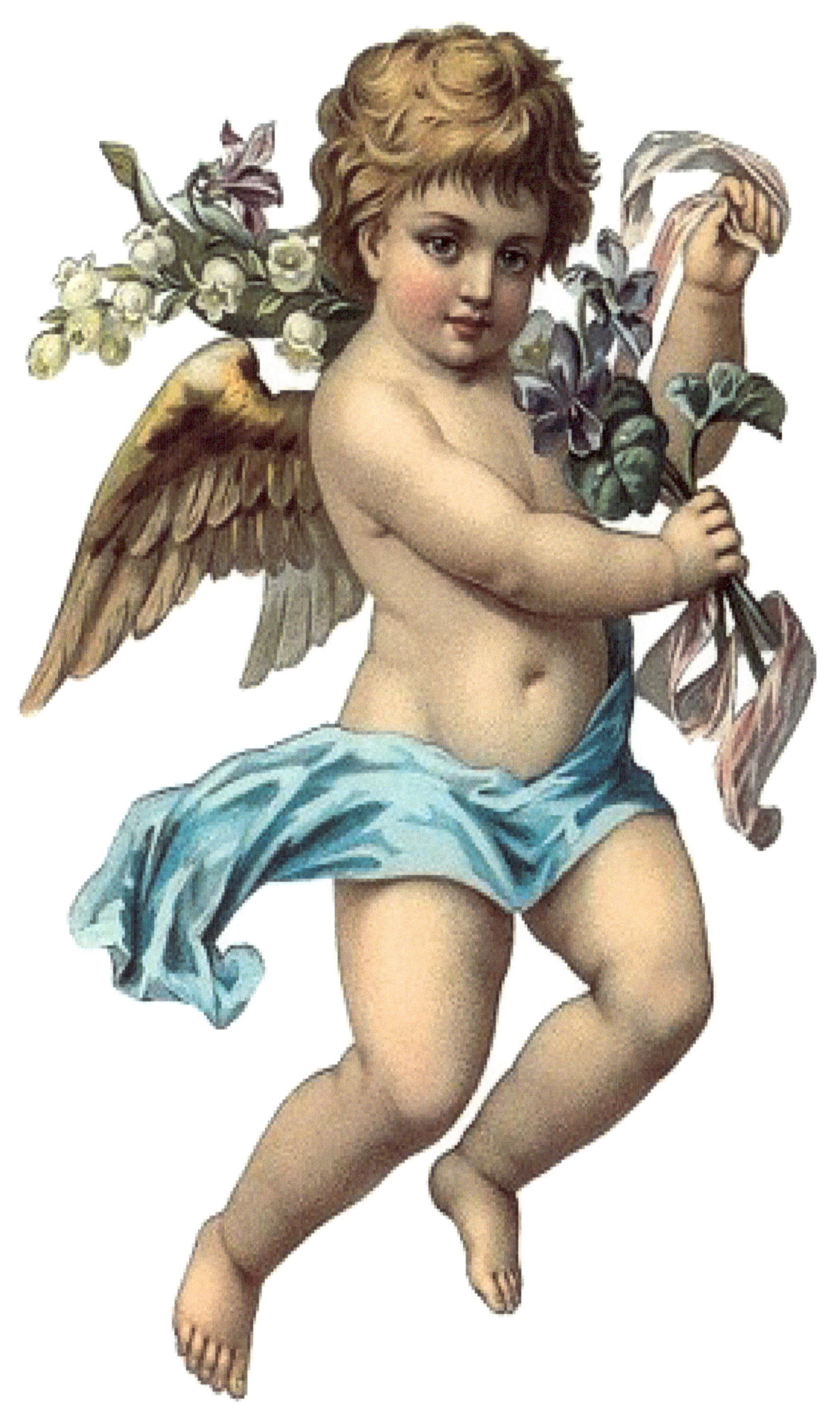

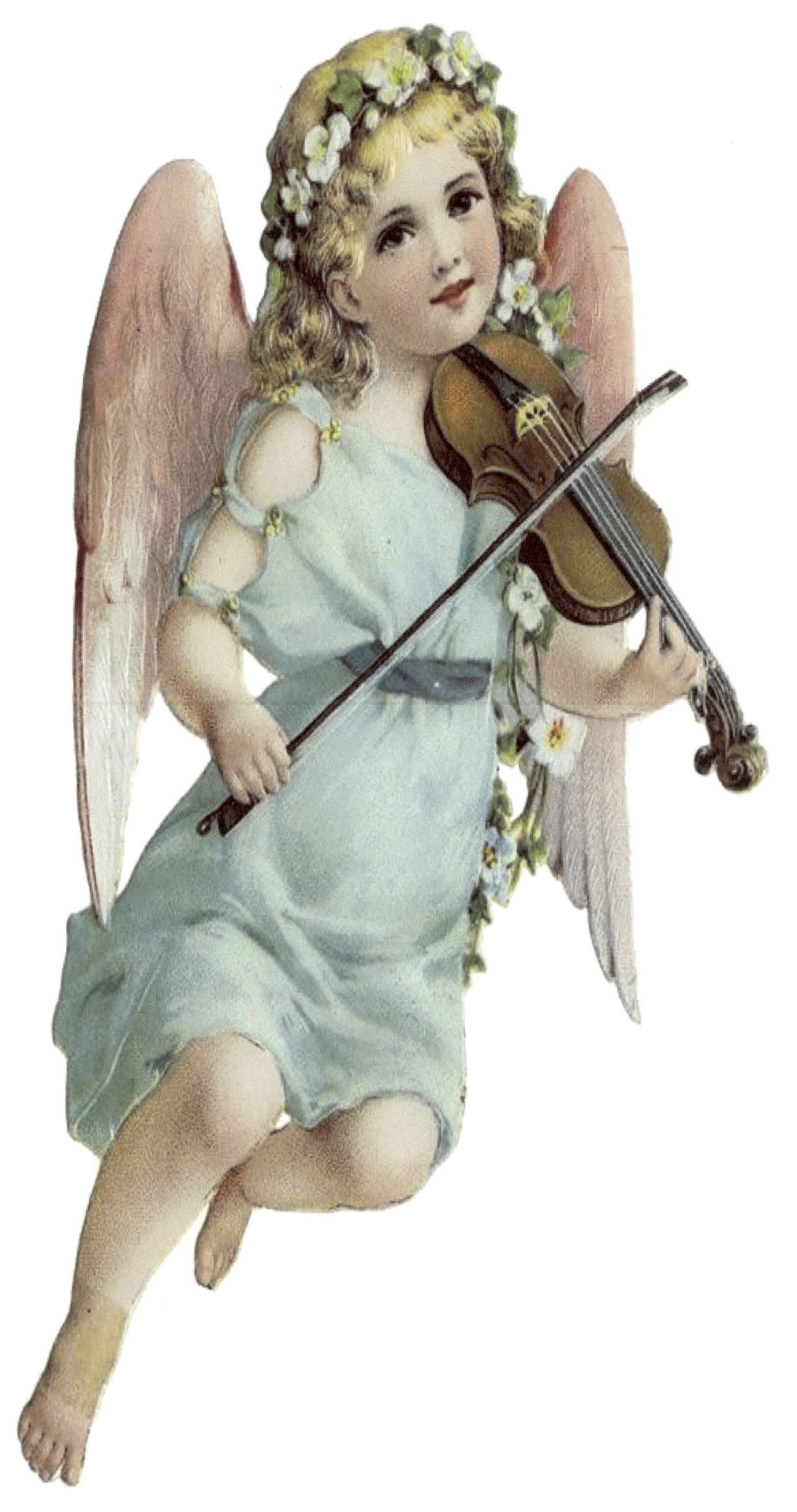

www.ingramcontent.com/pod-product-compliance
Lightning Source LLC
Chambersburg PA
CBHW051056180526
45172CB00002B/661